I Dare You!

by William H. Danforth

As a Man Thinketh

by James Allen

&

How to Live on 24 Hours a Day

by Arnold Bennett

© Copyright 2006 – BN Publishing

ISBN   9562913228

www.bnpublishing.com

info@bnpublishing.com

Printed in the U.S.A.

I DARE YOU!

By: WILLIAM H. DANFORTH

Founder and Former Chairman of the Board
Ralston Purina Company
St. Louis, Mo.

TABLE OF CONTENTS

FOREWORD

THOSE OF US who were associated with Mr. Danforth in business know this Dare idea works. Practically all the leaders in his great organization were boys who came from humble surroundings and were dared by him to high accomplishments. He dared most by his own daring example. Mr. Danforth always gave the best that was in him, whether he was guiding a great industry, traveling in a remote corner of the world, shooting ducks or playing with his grandchildren. The day ahead was always the most thrilling day in his life. The job at hand was always the most important one he had ever undertaken. He never gave less than his best.

Many years ago Mr. Danforth published "I Dare You" in a limited first edition for the benefit of his business, family and personal friends. Each book passed many times from one person to another. The idea spread and affected people of all ages and people in all walks of life. In one case, "I Dare You" inspired the sale of over $5,000,000 worth of insurance in a special day of the Life Underwriters' Association. The demand from salesmanagers, Y.M.C.A. secretaries, business executives, college organizations, vocational teachers, personnel and guidance workers, preachers - everyone whose aim it is to challenge men and women to superior accomplishment - soon exhausted the early editions. Now comes this twenty-ninth edition. Here is more than a book. It is a working pattern of life written out of a pioneer businessman's own rich experience. It is the challenge for which Today's Youth is waiting. It is a practical plan for action for everybody who wants to go somewhere, be somebody and be of service.

G.M. Philpott

AUTHOR'S PREFACE

I agree that a businessman should stick to business. But a proven four-fold program, plus a love for Youth, plus an inner urge-all *dare* me to write this book.

"I Dare You" is for the daring few who are headed somewhere. Those afraid to Dare might as well pass it up. It will weary the lazy because it calls for immediate action. It will bore the sophisticated, and amuse the skeptics. It will antagonize others. Some will not even know what it is all about. It will not be over-popular because it calls for courage, swift and daring. But in the eyes of you, one of *the priceless few,* I trust will come a renewal of purpose as you read on. You can be a bigger person than you are and I am going to prove it to you.

I am indebted beyond measure to Gordon M. Philpott, who has been of inestimable help in the writing and editing of "I Dare You." His keen insight, his rare judgment and his frank criticisms have helped make this book a labor of love instead of a drab task. I honor him as a close associate in business, but most of all I cherish him as an understanding friend.

W. H. D.

I DARE YOU!

"What I've dared I've willed;And what I've willed, I'll do!"

-Melville

I DARE YOU!

IT IS DIFFICULT to put a challenge on paper. I would rather look you straight in the eye and say, "I dare you!" In my mind that's exactly what I am doing. I am on one side of a table. You are on the other. I am looking across and saying: "I dare you!"

I Dare You, young man, you who come from a home of poverty - I dare you to have the qualities of a Lincoln.

I Dare You, heir of wealth and proud ancestry, with your generations of worthy stock, your traditions of leadership - I dare you to achieve something that will make the future point to you with even more pride than the present is pointing to those who have gone before you.

I Dare You, young mother, to make your life a masterpiece upon which that little family of yours can build. Strong women bring forth strong men.

I Dare You, boys and girls, to make life obey you, not you it. It is only a shallow dare to do the foolish things. I dare you to do the uplifting, courageous things.

I Dare You, young executive, to shoulder more responsibility joyously, to launch out into the deep, to build magnificently.

I Dare You, young author, to win the Nobel prize.

I Dare You, young researcher, to become a Microbe Hunter.

I Dare You, boy on the farm, to become a Master Farmer -A Hunger Fighter.

I Dare You, man of affairs, to have a "Magnificent Obsession."

I Dare You, Grandfather, with your roots deep in the soil and your head above the crowd catching the rays of the sun, to plan a daring program to crown the years of your life.

I Dare You, who think life is humdrum, to become involved. I dare you who are weak to be strong; you who are dull to be sparkling; you who are slaves to be kings.

I Dare You, whoever you are, to share with others the fruits of your daring. Catch a passion for helping others and a richer life will come back to you!

YOU CAN BE BIGGER THAN YOU ARE

As a small boy, before the time of drainage ditches, I lived in the country surrounded by swamplands. Those were days of chills and fever and malaria. When I came to the city to school, I was sallow-cheeked and hollow-chested. One of my teachers, George Warren Krall, was what we then called a health crank. We laughed at his ideas. They went in one ear and came out the other. But George Warren Krall never let up. One day he seemed to single me out personally. With flashing eye and in tones that I will never forget, he looked straight at me and said, "I dare you to be the healthiest boy in the class."

That brought me up with a jar. Around me were boys all stronger and more robust than I. To be the healthiest boy in the class when I was thin and sallow and imagined at least that I was full of swamp poisons! - the man was crazy. But I was brought up to take dares. His voice went on. He pointed directly at me. "I dare you to chase those chills and fevers out of your system. I dare you to fill your body with fresh air, pure water, wholesome food, and daily exercise until your cheeks are rosy, your chest full, and your limbs sturdy."

As he talked something seemed to happen inside me. My blood was up. It answered the dare and surged all through my body into tingling fingertips as though itching for battle.

I chased the poisons out of my system. I built a body that has equalled the strongest boys in that class, and has outlived and outlasted most of them. Since that day I haven't lost any time on account of sickness. You can imagine how often I have blessed that teacher who dared a sallow-cheeked boy to be the healthiest in the class.

Several years later, Henry Woods, one of our promising boys, pushed through the door of my office early one morning and stood facing me defiantly.

"I'm quitting," he said.

"What's the trouble, Henry?"

"Just this, I'm no salesman. I haven't got the nerve. I haven't got the ability, and I'm not worth the money you are paying me."

There was something splendid about the courage of a man who would so frankly admit failure to his boss. He couldn't do that without nerve. Suddenly my mind recalled the boyhood scene when a teacher dared a hollow-chested youngster to be strong. To Henry's surprise, instead of accepting his resignation, I looked him squarely in the eye and said:

"If I know how to pick men, you have sales stuff in you. I dare you, Henry Woods, to get out of this office, right now, and come back tonight with more orders than you have ever sold in any one day in your whole life."

He looked at me dumbfounded. Then a flash came into his eyes. It must have been the light of battle - the same something that had surged through me years before in answer to the teacher's dare. He turned and walked out of my office.

That night he came back. The defiant look of the early morning was replaced by the glow of victory. He had made the best record of his life. He had beaten his best and he has been beating his best ever since. Incidentally, I'll give you a secret of his life. In his quiet way he was one of the best helpers of young salesmen I ever knew. He thrives by giving his experience to others. The world is full of men like Henry Woods just waiting for a Dare.

In the American Youth Foundation Camps each summer I come into contact with hundreds of young people who possess qualities of leadership. A few years ago a young fellow, who was working as a mechanic in a large electrical firm, came to me much perplexed. He had been forced to go to work when he had finished high school. Later he saw boys with technical college training outstrip him. Sensing he had ability to be much more than a mechanic, I dared him to leave his job and go back to school. Again I saw that priceless light of battle leap into the eyes of a fighter. He had no money, but, somehow, he got to college, was graduated with honors, and today the might-have-been mechanic is a prominent electrical engineer. I can tell you one of the secrets of his life, too...he keeps on growing by sharing, because now he has a mania for helping others get an education.

These are brief pages taken from the book of my practical experiences. There are scores of other pages like them. Unfortunately, however, there are many pages that would tell that other story of those who have been dared to do the super thing, but in whose eyes the light to battle failed to gleam. But the "I Dare You" plan has worked with thousands. It will work with you. As your first step, I Dare You to read this book through tonight before YOU go to bed. Don't stop. Hurry through just to get its feel. Then if you are determined to be one of those priceless few leaders who are destined to reach the top, take this book as a program for adventuring toward your highest possibilities.

ARE YOU ONE OF THE PRICELESS FEW?

I am on a voyage of discovery. I search for those of you who will go on a great adventure. I am looking for you, one of the audacious few, who will face life courageously, ready to strike straight at the heart of anything that is keeping you from your best; you intrepid ones behind whom the world moves forward. To you, I am going to unfold a secret power that but few know how to use - the secret power of daring and sharing which carries with it tremendous responsibilities. Once you have it, you can never be the same again. Once it is yours, you can never rest until you have given it to others. And the more you give away the greater becomes your capacity to give. Deep down in the very fibre of your being you must light an urge that can never be put out. It will catch this side of your life, then that side. It will widen your horizons. It will light up unknown reserves and discover new capacities for living and growing. It will become, if you don't look out, a mighty conflagration that will consume your every waking hour. And to its blazing glory a thousand other lives will come for light and warmth and power.

It is going to take courage to let this urge possess you. My life in business and my contacts with young people have convinced me that the world is full of unused talents and latent ability. The reason these talents lie buried is that the individual hasn't the courage to dig them up and use them. Everybody should be doing better than he is, but only a few dare. Prospectors for gold tell us that gold is where they find it. It may be in the bed of a river or on the mountaintop. And prospectors for courage tell us the same thing. The one who dares may be found in a cottage or in a castle. But wherever you live, whoever you are, whatever you have or have not - if you dare, you are challenged to enlist in a great cause.

H. G. Wells tells how every human being can determine whether he has really succeeded in life. He says: "Wealth, notoriety, place, and power are no measure of success whatsoever. The only true measure of success is the ratio between what we might have done and what we might have been on the one hand, and the things we have made and the things we have made of ourselves on the other."

I want you to start a crusade in your life: to dare to be your best. I maintain that you are a better, more capable person than you have demonstrated so far. The only reason you are not the person you should be is you don't dare to be. Once you dare, once you stop drifting with the crowd and face life courageously, life takes on a new significance. New forces take shape within you. New powers harness themselves for your service.

Who wants to do unimportant and uninteresting things? Who even wants to gratify an ambition that has grown into a passion for fame and fortune? To desire something permanent in life, to develop your gifts to the largest possible use - that's your dare. You have a wealth of possibilities, but maybe up to this time you have lacked a definite aim. You have a gun and plenty of ammunition. Now I dare you to aim at something worthy of the best that is in you.

My practical experience has convinced me that inner growth and broadening personality come from daring and sharing. You dare to use the talents you have. You find yourself growing stronger - physically, mentally, socially and spiritually. You multiply your daring a hundred-fold by sharing its fruits. You give your life away and, behold! A richer life comes back to you. This principle works through all of life: Our most valuable possessions are those which can be shared without lessening; those which, when shared, multiply. Our least valuable possessions are those which, when divided, are diminished.

Old or young, rich or poor, man or woman, if you are one of those audacious few willing to dare and then to share, then come with me. This book is written for you. I promise you adventure. I promise you a more abundant life.

"All who joy would win
Must share it.
Happiness was born a twin."

I DARE YOU TO ADVENTURE

Before we start on the great adventure, let's be dead sure we want to take it. Unless one is interested and enthusiastic he would not even want to go on a picnic let alone start on a journey destined to bulk large in life's affairs. When our appetites have a sharp edge, we enjoy our meals.

Adventure means living to the full.

You will want to start when you know how much happiness it will bring you. Some of my young friends, who are freedom-loving pleasure seekers, maintain that drifting along with life is happiness, that resistance is vulgar, that self-indulgence is self-expression. Rot! I take issue with them. The line of least resistance makes crooked rivers and crooked men. Each fish that battles upstream is worth ten that loaf in lazy bays.

True, the masses of people prefer the easy way. Old ways require no effort. Physically or mentally lazy people do not want to adjust themselves. But they have never tasted the thrill of victory. I remember once during the First World War a captain was wounded in No Man's Land when returning from a raid. Snipers and machine gunners shot across a defiant barrage as though daring anyone to come and get his prostrate body. The company commander called for two volunteers to undertake the dangerous mission of rescuing the wounded man. The whole company stepped forward. The major chose the two men with the most deserving record and longest service. Out on their bellies they crawled and brought in their captain. In crack regiments it is a privilege to dare and to give. There are no big thrills in the trenches. But just poke your head over the parapet and you'll find excitement enough. Your days won't be humdrum when you lift your head above the crowd.

"I Dare You to Adventure" is my message to those red-blooded young leaders I meet every summer at the American Youth Foundation Camp in Michigan. Every year there come to this camp hundreds and hundreds of boys and girls, young men and young women, who aspire to be leaders. During certain hours, the whole Camp resounds with the keen competition these young people have in striving to best one another in a game of baseball, in a diving contest, or in climbing to some lofty height. Or at another time of the day they are just as intense, just as interested, in a mental training program - because these young people are to be future leaders and their trained directors have learned the art of making their mental program just as interesting and absorbing as their physical program. At night in the council circle each tribe competes against each other in entertainment features. Each future leader learns the art of expressing himself, entertaining his fellow campers; he handles his personality in such a way it attracts, leads and influences others. During a devotional program these hundreds of young people are just as absorbed in expressing and developing their spiritual selves as they are on the athletic field or in the study room or in the council circle. These young campers have realized that all sides of life can be equally interesting. Show me boys and girls anywhere who enjoy life more than do these. "My own self, at my very best, all the time," is the Camp Motto. They are daring to live at their best, following a Four-square program, and they are having a glorious time doing it. Living right has a lasting kick in it. Living wrong is a bit of foam on top, that's all.

In the spirit of a crusader, life is a glorious adventure. If you jump out of bed in the morning full of fight, daring people or circumstances to depress you, you are on the road to victory. If you face problems aggressively, they are half solved already. If you aspire to larger responsibilities, they will meet you half way.

But how to dare, you ask. That is coming. First, it is necessary to agree that living aggressively changes the whole complexion of life. So many are preys to fear. You fear losing your job. You fear sickness or hard times or failure. But remember, courage is not the absence of fear, it is the conquest of it. Not until you dare to attack will you master your fears.

And why dare? Because unless you dare you cannot win. Deep down in every heart is the desire to be somebody, to get somewhere. But so often we sit waiting for the opportunity. I have found opportunities do not come to those who wait. They are captured by those who attack.

Perhaps you are sitting back in your chair reading this and saying, "It is all very well for him to say that. But my circumstances are different. It is impossible for me to dare." I challenge that thought in your mind. I know it is your deadly enemy. Because of it, you, more than others, must dare. The humdrum life is the one most in need of adventure. You can cure your weakness by vigorous action. Start something! Break a window, if necessary.

I am daring you to think bigger, to act bigger, and to be bigger. And I am promising you a richer life and a more exciting life if you do. I am showing you a world teeming with opportunity. The rewards for daring were never so rich or so plentiful. Science, religion, business, education - all are looking for the man who dares face life, to attack rather than defend.

Before you read further, be honest with yourself. What do you think of life anyway? What do you think of yourself? Are you satisfied that you are carrying responsibility equal to your capacity? Are you contented to have posterity look at your life so a far and say, "That is all he was capable of?" Or, are you one of the priceless few, one of those with a restless feeling that some day you are going to climb to your rightful place of leadership? That some day you are going to create something worthy of your best? If this is your attitude then my voyage of discovery is not in vain. You are the volunteer for whom I am looking. Then make that "some day" you have been waiting for, today.

I DARE YOU TO DO THINGS

In France, during those dark World War I days of 1918, I marveled at the way my old army comrade, Colonel E. L. Daley of the Sixth Engineers, got things done. I began to understand better when I heard what he had said to his own boys in America when he was bidding them goodbye. "Boys," said he, "your name is Daley, and Daley stands for the ability to do things!" No longer will you step aside to let crusaders go by. Others shall step aside for you because you are now a crusader. You have the ability to do things. You know where you are going. The world makes way for the man who knows where he is going. Streets are crowded, traffic is jammed, a fire engine is coming - everything makes way for it. True, moments of weakness and depression and laziness are going to assail you. But that is the time for battle. One forward step, one swift constructive action, will send these enemies scurrying to cover.

I remembered reading a newspaper account of a mother killing a bear with an axe when it threatened her baby. A woman cannot kill a bear - but she did.

Gordon Philpott tells me of a Canadian street car conductor, who rose to be a General in the First World War. The conductor did not know he could command men, but he could.

Not many years ago a young man was working as a section hand on a railroad. His thoroughness won him an opportunity to work for a few days in the shipping office. During those few days the superintendent asked the young substitute clerk for some vital facts and figures. The young man did not know anything about bookkeeping, but he worked three days and three nights without sleep and had the facts ready when the superintendent returned. The same daring which made him always willing to tackle the bigger job even though he knew nothing about it, the same thoroughness which has characterized everything he has done, have been stepping stones to higher and higher responsibilities. Today he is vice-president of our own company.

Until he was nineteen, a young Kentucky mountain boy had never been out of his own county and had never seen a railroad. He rose to become Chairman of the Board of one of our largest Western banks and a Past-President of the American Bankers' Association. In time he was elected a Trustee of Berea College, that marvelous Kentucky school of three thousand mountain boys and girls. "This is the greatest honor of my life," said this now grown-up country boy, in humbly accepting this place of service and responsibility. Experience had taught him that real satisfaction is not riches or fame but in giving one's self for others.

An Alabama miner, working with his hands, realized the lack of an education. He studied by candlelight. He "read" law a bit. When gold was struck in the Yukon, he was swept off his feet. He dared to go. In the Yukon he found his fortune in the bowels of the earth. He also found something far greater. Lost in a driving snowstorm, in this cold, bleak Northland, he saw in the distance a shining cross set up by the missionaries and that vision dared him to follow a new Master. He found a new Life.

The other day I saw a creative country boy, supposedly lacking in culture, poise, and social graces, hold his own in a brilliant gathering, to his own amazement as well as mine.

I know a successful but modest businessman, who, when called on in an emergency, discovered in himself a rich capacity for spiritual uplift to those around him.

I can give you all these men's names. I know them well. They found they had capacity and used it.

Wars and emergencies discover many unopened doors in people's lives. Why not declare war? Why not put a bomb under your capacities? Why not force a crisis? Without some such incentives to stir souls to action, the mother never knows her strength, the street car conductor never discovers the General, the section hand, the miner, the country boys, the business man, live and die without realizing the sleeping giants within them. The purpose of this book is, first,

17

to help you discover what living tools you have to work with, and, secondly, to dare you to use all of them. Launch out into the deep. Walter B Pitkin, author of "The Psychology of Achievement," says that thousands of young people can double, tripple, and quadruple their effectiveness simply by being aroused to Creative Audacity. But, alas, many lack courage because, at a still deeper level, they lack the immense energies which a daring program demands. He tells me that he used to train boxers and often he would find a brilliantly clever boxer fail to rise in the sport. "He lacked the punch" because he showed physical fatigue long before less skilled rivals did and in the long grueling run, lost.

It is a tragedy indeed to see an ambitious person striving after some goal he has neither the energy nor ability to reach. But it is a thousand times greater tragedy and, alas, a more common one, to see Generals and Vice-presidents, spiritual and mental leaders, passing by unnoticed as street car conductors, section hands, and bellhops.

But what is it, you ask, that turns a streetcar conductor into a General? What is the method? Did he just go to the war, dare to become a General, then stick out his chest and wait for the medals to be pinned on? No, sir! Generals aren't made that way. The fact is, several things took place inside that streetcar conductor before he became a General. Before the war, he had been living in a narrow conductor world-eating, sleeping, mingling with a few friends and collecting fares. Suddenly he stepped into a new world: Horizons were pushed back on all sides. The sleeping giants within him stirred and awakened.

What were these sleeping giants? The first was a physical one. Where he had spent most of his waking hours in the stuffy, stodgy atmosphere of a streetcar, he now galloped about on a horse, had physical instructors punch in his stomach and push up his chest, got plenty of exercise, lived out of doors, ate simple food. He found vibrant health and abundant strength at his disposal. Then his mental life broadened. He bunked in a tent next to a college professor. He worked on a gun crew beside a civil engineer. Their minds quickened his. He saw the great cities of London and Paris. He went to an artillery school and found he could learn to do higher mathematics as well as add up fares. He had only needed to use one corner of his brain to be a conductor. Now almost every new experience demanded that another compartment be opened and aired. In the third place, he had the gift of making all kinds of people like him - men and boys in the army from every walk of life, fighting with a great purpose in their hearts. Back at home his streetcar contacts were only of the meagerest sort. One priceless day he discovered that he had a new power: the ability to lead people. Laborers, college men, business men recognized him as the one to march in front. A streetcar conductor never had that opportunity. He was always in the rear. And, finally, although he never made any religious profession, for the first time in his life he was filled with a passion for a great moral cause.

But why, you ask, didn't all the other streetcar conductors become Generals? They were thrown into the same environment. The answer is obvious. Either they didn't have the capacity to be a General, or they didn't dare to use the capacity they had. This one found within himself undreamed-of physical powers, unused mental gifts, decided ability to influence people, and a depth of character which was the rock on which his success was built. And, having discovered this four-sided life, he had the courage and daring to make it broaden, deepen, and rise above the lives of those around him.

The same is true of the country boy who was nineteen before he saw a railroad. But he made up his mind that some day he would ride in the cars and see the world. Only a country boy? Yes, but with the capacity of a man able to carry world problems on his shoulders. For nineteen years on the farm he had been building a strong physical foundation. Then, when opportunity came, he found each successive year developing mental, social, and spiritual resources, until he received the highest honor in the banking world.

What are the hidden resources to look for? What are these sleeping giants within us? There are four of them: the physical, the mental, the social, and the spiritual. Life cannot be complete unless we develop all four sides. Each side that is developed in turn stimulates the other three sides. "All for one and one for all." Life's Musketeers work together for one common end. All down the pages of history great lives have been telling us this secret of the four-fold life. Pick them out of any age, from any line of endeavor. They all tell the same story - that progress is a complete program coming out of all four sides of life. St. Luke gives us eloquent evidence of just one little peep into the four-fold development of the greatest success of all time: "And Jesus increased in wisdom and stature and in favor with God and man."

Now listen to Sir Wilfred Grenfell's message: "Man must play, work, love and worship to get the most out of life." Read his words again.

How dare you have within yourself these four-fold capacities and not use them?

That is the first principle that I want thoroughly to fix in your mind: that life is a four-sided affair, that your daring program is going to lead you into physical adventures, mental adventures, social adventures, spiritual adventures. You have not one, but four lives to live, a four-fold opportunity to grow. A body, a brain, a heart, and a soul - these are our living tools. To use them is not a task. It is a golden opportunity. To find new capacities within you is not robbing you of any pleasure. It is bringing new treasures into every waking hour. It is helping you touch life at all angles, absorb strength from all contacts, pour out power on all fronts.

And here is another interesting thing. The more you pour out, the more you find to pour. The more of Life's treasures you keep to yourself, the less you have. The more you share with others, the more you have yourself. One of Life's great rules is this: The more you give, the more you get. I am not trying to soar in the clouds. This principle is the result of my own practical experience. I know that if you dare to use the talents you have you find yourself growing stronger physically, mentally, socially, spiritually, and that you multiply them a hundred-fold by sharing their fruits. You give your life away and behold! A richer life comes back to you.

I repeat Life's great principle. *Our most valuable possessions are those which can be shared without lessening; those which when shared multiply. Our least valuable possessions are those which when divided are diminished.*

NOW FOR THE START

Suppose you were to draw a picture of your life as you are living it today. How near four-square would it be?

Would it look like this?

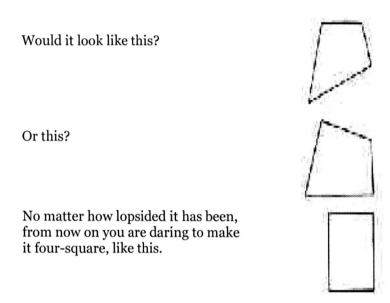

Or this?

No matter how lopsided it has been, from now on you are daring to make it four-square, like this.

I have been taught that a pencil and a piece of paper help clarify the mind. I want so to burn this four-square idea into your brain that it will be a part of you. I won't be able to put across the completeness of the four-square life unless I get you to make definite moves for yourself.

On the left, at the top of the next page, I have drawn my four-square checker. Now won't you take a sheet of paper and draw yours? Make all sides equal. Write "Physical" on the left-hand side, "Mental" at the top and "Social" on the right-hand side, "Religious" under the base. Then in the middle write "My Checker" and sign your initials.

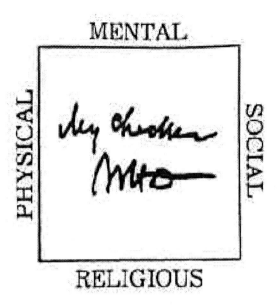

MENTAL

PHYSICAL

SOCIAL

RELIGIOUS

No plan is worth the paper it is printed on unless it starts you doing something. There is too much telling in this life and not enough doing. Unless you have actually drawn and labeled your checker for yourself, even though the four-fold plan has only been outlined, you are not ready for the next step.

After you have drawn your checker, look at it well. Photograph it on your brain. There you have the picture of the Magic Square - the symbol of the richer, fuller life; the emblem you are to follow in your daring crusade.

The chapters that follow give a definite program for the daring few who are determined to tap all of their inner resources. If you don't feel the urge to Dare don't waste your time to go on. If you lack courage or faith the following pages will not help you. But if you are able and willing to do and dare then immediately assume the offensive.

The day of defending your present possessions is gone. From now on you are not going to worry about holding your job. Put the worry on the fellow above you about holding his. From this day onward wrong things are put on the defense. You have marshalled right things for the attack. Your eyes are turned toward your strength, not your weakness. Henceforth you will wake in the morning thinking of ways to do things, rather than reasons why they can't be done. When Henry Ford wanted to get an unbreakable glass for his new models he wouldn't see any of the experts. They knew too many reasons why it couldn't be done. "Bring me eager young fellows who do not know the reasons why unbreakable glass cannot be made. Give this problem to ambitious young fellows who think nothing is impossible." He got unbreakable glass.

> *"That tower of strength*
> *Which stood four-square*
> *To all winds that blew."*
>
> *-Tennyson*

I DARE YOU TO BE STRONG

I often wonder what would have happened to me if my old school teacher, George Warren Krall, hadn't dared me to be the healthiest boy in my class. Certainly I would not have dared what I have tried to accomplish. Sickness robs us of time, courage and money. Wealth can't buy health but health can buy wealth.

Many a young man today, starting out on a road he hopes will lead to success, looks at men of affairs who have gone before him and tries to select those attributes which will lead him into that charmed circle of successful men. He will find, however, it is pretty difficult to determine just what are the essentials of a successful career. Some leaders are tall men, some are short men; some are men from the country, some from the city. Some are men with college background, others are men whose only schooling was "reading, 'riting and 'rithmetic." Some are geniuses, some are pluggers. In an issue of Fortune, I read an article that gives a brief word picture of a dozen or more of the leading executives of the General Motors Corporation. Each man is a distinct personality - no two came from the same environment, but I did find one common attribute of every single one of them. That is *energy*. I think if you look for the propelling force of any successful executive, you will find it is energy. True, you may find an occasional man who has succeeded in spite of the lack of energy, but for every one of such you will find twenty or thirty have succeeded because of it.

Every time I met Walter Pitkin he fired at me questions such as these:

1) Have I capacity for hard work?
2) Can I keep everlastingly at it?
3) Have I sustained "Pep and Punch"?
4) Do I maintain a high batting average?
5) What is my ability to spurt?

These are questions that stir me to the depths. How can you maintain energy without health? In our own company, every employee in both office and field must pass a physical examination before he can come on our payroll. Afterwards he must pass a rigid physical examination once a year. Why? Because a fit employee does things. He's worth more than an unfit one.

I like the way Huxley expresses this game of life: ". . . It is very plain that the life, the fortune and the happiness of everyone of us do depend upon our knowing something of the rules of a game infinitely more difficult and complicated than chess. It is a game which has been played for untold ages, every man and woman of us being one of the two players in a game of his or her own. The chessboard is the world, the pieces are the phenomena of the universe, the rules of the game are what we call the laws of nature. The player on the other side is hidden from us. We know that his play is always fair, just and patient. But also we know to our cost that he never overlooks a mistake or makes the smallest allowance for ignorance. To the man who plays well the highest stakes are paid with that sort of overflowing generosity with which the strong show delight in strength. And one who plays ill is checkmated, without haste but without remorse."

If you were trying to make the football team this fall or the basketball team next winter, would you object to eating at the training table, getting regular sleep and going through the rigorous but stimulating body-building program that would make you fit when the crucial test came? Every day is a crucial test in the game of life. The longer you live the better will you understand that fact. Every time you take liberties with your physical strength, such as eating or drinking things that do not agree with you, or losing sleep, you will find that some day you will

pay the price when you need the ability to spurt, or maintain a high batting average, or need strength
for that extra pep and punch when all those around you are weakening.

Life is a bigger game than football or basketball, but the same rules maintain. If you keep strong, physically fit, full of energy and enthusiasm, you are the man whom life's coach is going to pick when the winning touchdown is needed. But if you do not follow the rules, if you become indifferent in the care of your physical strength, then the coach will yank you out of the game and put a more capable person in your place.

Health is the foundation for individual success. Health is one of the greatest assets industry looks for, and health is the foundation of a nation's progress. In 1877, in one of his memorable statements, Disraeli declared that: "The health of the people is really the foundation upon which all their happiness and all their power as a state depend. It is quite possible for a kingdom to be inhabited by an able and active population. You may have successful manufacturers and you may have a productive agriculture; the arts may flourish, architecture may cover your land with temples and palaces, you may have even material powers to defend and support all these acquisitions; you may have arms of precision, fleets of warships. But if the population of the country is stationary or yearly diminishing - if, while it diminishes in number it diminishes also in stature, in strength, that country is doomed. The health of the people is, in my opinion, the first duty of a statesman."

As I write this chapter the world is passing through an economic depression. Everybody is being called upon to bear extra burdens. There is a crisis in every nation, in every business, in every household. Woe to the nation or business or individual who have no health reserves! Nerves snap, tempers explode, bodies and minds give way under the strain unless they can call up physical reinforcements. How fortunate the nation, business or individual which has a sturdy constitution capable of shouldering the extra load without faltering.

When leaders command, bodies obey. "Body, what can you do with flabby muscles and faulty digestion? How can you arrive anywhere if you get tired and your energy peters out? That hollow chest and those drooping shoulders will never get you to the top of the ladder. About face! Muscles strong! Chest up! Head erect!" It is difficult at first, but soon the sheer joy of vigorous health amply rewards you for daring to be strong and well.

Sadly enough, it is oftentimes necessary for us to lose our health before we appreciate it. Youth, for instance, is a spendthrift of health and strength because there is such a surplus. It isn't taken seriously. But I am daring you crusaders to take health seriously. I have seen ambitious young men right on the threshold of a striking success crack because of ill health. That's too heavy a price to pay for the privilege of being a spendthrift of health and energy. Why not stay on Mount Health? It is a laborious climb back after you have fallen down the side. Besides, a ride in the ambulance below isn't the most pleasant thing.

One of Technology's most prominent graduates, addressing a small group of students, talked almost solely on the necessity of safeguarding health. He stressed health so strongly, he said, because of his personal acquaintance with so many men whose success had been snatched away because of physical failure just when they were about to reap the reward of a long struggle.

Keeping fit is not a tedious job. Treating your body with the ordinary care you give your automobile or your dog is not a nuisance. Giving your body the stimulation of good, wholesome food is more fun than doping it with artificial stimulants. Again I challenge the scoffers who say that living right is not more thrilling than living wrong. You can keep yourself fit and enjoy doing it. Make it a game. Make it the hard thing to do not to eat right, not to take regular exercises, not to get the proper amount of sleep. You can play bridge until midnight, but not every night and feel rested in the morning. Keep caught up on your sleep. Anybody can ride every place in an automobile. My car is a convenience, but I walk my mile a day because I feel the better for it. It's my program.

My physical life has been a happy one. Why shouldn't it be happy? Good health makes happiness. My friends envy me because I have never lost a day at the office on account of illness. Yet the same friends think I am a faddist on health. And I am a faddist! It pays. Good health has been the most profitable, most enjoyable fad I know. Some faddists don't exercise and don't bother with regular hours. Personally, I would rather have my fad than theirs.

There is no secret to good health other than just plain, good common sense. You wouldn't let your automobile go along, week after week, month after month, without the proper mixture of oil and gas and overhauling. Why, under heaven, do you expect your body to carry on without at least the same consideration? You wouldn't keep a dog or a horse cooped up in a stall all day without a chance to stretch its legs. Then why expect to avoid trouble if you treat your own priceless machine in such a manner? Everybody knows these things, but so few do anything about it. I have never been able to understand why people are not willing to pay the small price for good health.

I don't particularly enjoy getting out of bed in the morning and touching the floor twenty times and twisting my liver fifty times and stretching to the heavens for posture. I don't like these exercises any more than I like to shave. But I wouldn't appear at my office with a bristling beard. That would discount me in the eyes of my associates. I don't like exercising and I don't like shaving, but I'm going to do both. A Scotch friend once told me he didn't like the taste of liquor. "Then why drink it?" I asked him. "For the effect," he replied. Just so, I don't particularly like the immediate taste of morning exercises, but I do like the effect. Even my Scotch friend will agree that exercising is a lot more permanent-and cheaper, too.

I dare you to exercise! Keep yourself fit and enjoy the consequences. Attack it in the right attitude. Let me illustrate:

John and George both begin to take exercises. John crawls out of bed in the morning thinking, "Oh, darn, I've got to take those exercises", and he goes unwillingly through them. In a few days or weeks he is fudging, dropping off one and then two. One night he is out late and next morning is so sleepy he satisfies his "conscience" that the extra few minutes' sleep will do him more good than the exercises. Soon a hundred excuses are found for not taking those exercises. John stops, feeling half honest and sincere in doing so.

But now consider George. He believes that exercises every morning will make him a better man all day. He thoroughly establishes that thought in his mind. He knows that not to take those exercises puts a burden on him for the rest of the day. When the alarm clock rings, two voices whisper in his ear. One says, "Don't take those exercises. What's the use?" The other voice says, "All right, George, now is your opportunity to start the biggest day of the week. Stretch up those arms, because today you must grow more than yesterday. Squeeze that liver. Get your blood in circulation. A strong body is necessary if you are to tackle that bigger job." Which voice is he going to heed? Then when he, like John, is out late at night, morning finds him with this attitude: "Not so much sleep as usual last night. Brain a bit slower. All the more need for physical strength to meet the opportunities which may come my way. Up-and-at my exercises. No slipping for me." Which voice are you going to heed?

I have a young friend who smoked too much and who refused to take daily exercises. "I hate standing over myself like a policeman," he told me, "always telling myself I must not do this or I must do that. I don't believe it would do me any good to cut out smoking, that is, if I had to threaten myself with a club. To drive myself to exercise every morning might build me up physically, but it would certainly wear me down mentally. I like to do the things I enjoy doing."

Perfectly right, too. Most people do. But I suggested he should make himself enjoy doing the things he did not like to do. That sounded like a paradox and he laughed at me, but soon after his doctor showed him how it could be done. He became dangerously ill and the doctor who pulled him through the critical stage said, "Now go ahead and smoke all you want, but when you light a cigarette, just say to yourself, 'This will make it harder for me to get back my full strength.' and when you get up in the morning say, 'I won't take any exercise and I'll soon be back in bed.' " Pretty shrewd judge of human nature, that doctor. He knew his patient only did the things he enjoyed doing. He made it hard to enjoy wrong things and easy to enjoy right things. Habits rule most of our actions, but they are mostly mental, and a changed mental attitude can change a bad habit to a good one.

Long ago I discovered a daily prescription that agreed with me. The old bootmaker, mentioned by Hinsdale in his essay, "Atmospheric Air in Relation to Tuberculosis", has this to say about walking:

"The best medicine! Two miles of oxygen three times a day. This is not only the best, but is cheap and pleasant to take. It suits all ages and constitutions. It is patented by infinite wisdom, sealed with a signet divine. It cures cold feet, hot heads, pale faces, feeble lungs, and bad tempers. If two or three take it together, it has a still more striking effect. It has often been known to reconcile enemies, settle matrimonial quarrels, and bring reluctant parties to a state of double blessedness. This medicine never fails. Spurious compounds are found in large towns; but get into the country lanes, among green fields, or on the mountain top, and you have it in perfection as prepared in the great laboratory of Nature."

I make it a practice to walk a mile a day. For the same reason, I drink eight glasses of water every day, get seven or eight hours regular sleep, and generally try to obey the common sense laws of Nature that make me feel better. I obey them, not because I have aches and pains, but because I want tingling blood and wide open eyes and sound sleep and a healthy appetite. I go to a doctor twice a year, not because there is anything wrong with me, but to make sure that nothing will be wrong.

If our theory, that valuable possessions, when shared, multiply, is sound, how can we use the buoyance of our physical life? That glow of personal health – can it be shared? Which one of us doesn't buck up when we come into the presence of a man with head erect, shoulders square, chest up? Does he lose by having good health radiate from every fibre of his being? Not a bit of it. As he helps others, his passion for strength grows.

My friend, Dr. Joel E. Goldthwait, has done marvels in building strong men and women. He, himself, is a living example of his theories. Magnificent of posture - tall, straight, deep of chest, clear of eye, ruddy of cheek - he shares his splendid self with his patients. And into every patient Dr. Goldthwait instills a burning desire to build up others. Inevitably, as we carry the gospel of health to others, the more abundant health we possess ourselves.

Before you go on your next adventure, you will want to map out a pretty definite physical program. Nobody can do this for you. It is entirely up to you whether you succeed or fail on this pPhysical battlefront. Abundant health is such a luxury! Energy is such an asset in business. Physical strength is the backbone of success and happiness in every walk of life. Now you must prove that you are in earnest and want to grow strong. I know from experience that your most sinister enemy is a desire to put off the fight. Unless you begin your Physical Dare program now, you might as well chuck this book.

I have suggested a few things which have helped me physically during my lifetime. All are simple rules, easy to carry out, and have been the powerful contributing factors to the splendid health which I have always enjoyed. Eight hours sleep. Open windows. Regular daily exercise, morning and night. Eat the things that agree with me, but not overeat. Walk my mile a day. Open air every noontime and on vacations. Plenty of sunshine. Practice simple rules of posture which make me feel better. Besides, the man who walks straight and sits straight, I believe thinks straight. And lastly, I have talked health to our employees, to my family and to everybody I meet. As I told you before, they consider me a faddist but I expect to be urging good health on everybody in sight until the day I die.

Please don't think I am trying to give you a complete program for your physical development. That is for you and your doctor or some other competent person to work out. All I want is to put the thought in your head and the urge in your heart to dare something physically. If you have determined to beat your best physically, in the next twelve months, why not ask yourself these questions:

1. Am I in good physical condition now?

2. If not, what am I going to do about it?

3. What weakness will I overcome this year?

For example: bad posture, hollow chest,

overweight, underweight, lack of sleep, bad

digestion, constipation, headaches.

4. How?

5. What is my big physical Dare for this year ahead?

6. Will I store up enough surplus energy to carry me through my "Beat My Best" year? I will need strong reserves. Can't afford to weaken in the last round. That's when my enemies falter. Extra energy, extra punch!

7. What will I definitely do about this?

8. Will I stick to this Dare until I win out?

I am going to dare to suggest that after answering the above questions on a sheet of paper, you decide on a very definite program. One of my associates who in one year made the greatest physical progress of his life, gave me the following sights which turned a defeat into a victory.

Eliminate illness of last year.	Have thorough physical examination on my birthday, February 15th, and have every recommendation of the doctor carried out before March 30th.	Examined February 15 th. Doctor recomended dental treatment. Done March 10th.
	Eating meat only once a day recomended	
Taper off and finally cut out smoking for one month.	No smoking during Lent.	Succeeded.
Get more sleep.	Average seven hours a night; better still, eight.	Yes.
Double the amount of fresh air I get.	Sleep with windows open.	
Correct constipation.	Exercise 10 minutes every morning and evening.	Missed only two days.
Correct stooped shoulders.	Put a sign "Don't buckle at the waist" on my desk. Practice "abdomen in, hips flat, chest up, chin in" at least five times each day by standing back against a wall - hips, shoulders, head, all touching the wall.	Yes. December 3rd.
	Walk a mile every day. Don't say you haven't time. Do it.	Yes.
Have regular walking program.	Read book on Diet and Health and profit by it.	Ok.
Balance my diet.	Eat some good wholesome cereal every day.	Yes.
	Eat meat only one a day and a green salad every day.	Yes.
	Cut out desserts at noon.	

In order to make you posture-conscious, I want to add a few illustrations and suggest three simple exercises[1].

When a man takes a chair in my office and slides down on his backbone, I feel like yanking him up by the back of the neck.

When a man sits straight I believe he can think straight.

When I pass a man with head erect, chin in, shoulders square, abdomen in, he is such an inspiration to me that I straighten up, too. Straighten Up!

When a girl sits opposite me at meal time with shoulders slouched down and all buckled up at the waist, I can hardly keep from saying, "Straighten up!"

---

[1] Taken form Mr. Danforth's book "Growth."

Johnny has good posture

Susie has poor posture

(A) The "Stand Tall" Posture. This is the aristocratic bearing. You know this man is happy and successful.

(B) The "Watch Out" Posture. This posture is still good but slipping. It probably belongs to one who has always stood tall, but has now begun to take things easy.

(C) The "Trouble Ahead" Posture. This belongs to the person who never remembers to stand or sit straight. He slumps at the desk, slouches when he walks and curls up in an easy chair in the evening.

(D) The "Trouble Is Here" Posture. This person has gone so long without straightening up that there is a complete let down in his muscles. He has indigestion, constipation, rheumatism and goodness knows what not.

In which of these four classes do you belong? Certainly you can't afford to guess, because most of us think our posture is better than it really is. After you take your bath tomorrow morning, stand in front of a full-length mirror or place a light so that it casts your shadow on a white wall. Get your wife or roommate to take the four figures shown above and tell you in which one you belong. Mark your height on a wall because you will notice in the above figures that good posture makes you taller. If you improve your posture you will actually "grow" in stature. What could be more fitting for a growth year than to increase your height?

Here's another test. Stand up straight to a wall with toes touching. If your posture is correct the wall will just touch your chest but no other part of your body and it will miss your nose about an inch. Mark your height on the wall.

Three Simple Daily Posture Exercises

Don't expect to jump a class in posture over night. It took several years to "get" your present posture. Allow at least a few months to show improvement. Remember, posture is largely a matter of mind. If you can remember to straighten up, you will. In order to help you remember, try these three simple exercises every day.

1. Abdomen In
Before you get out of bed in the morning, pull the pillow from under your head, lie flat on your back, put both hands on back of neck and pull in your abdomen. Try to pull all of your intestines up under your ribs. Do this ten times. Do it ten more times before going to sleep at night.

2. Stand Tall
Jump out of bed, put both hands on top of your head and stretch yourself up as high as you can, hold it a second, then relax. Repeat this ten times, then again at night before going to bed.

3. Walk at Attention
The first block that you walk after leaving your house, pull yourself to attention -chin in, chest up, abdomen in - and walk as though you were passing General Pershing in a reviewing stand. "Push out your third vest button." Next week do it two blocks. If you drive to work, take a walk at noon "at attention." After a while you will get the habit of straightening up whenever you start to walk. You will find, too, that walking straight makes you feel like "cutting loose" at a brisk pace which means more air in the lungs, better blood circulation and better health.

I DARE YOU TO THINK CREATIVELY

Look here, Mind, you can't command unless you first learn to obey. You can't direct others without training. K.P. minds stay in the kitchen. The mind of a General makes one a General. Victories are thought out before they are fought out on the battlefield. What do you mean, Mind, by thinking on a low plane when I am daring to set High Achievement as my goal?

In "Pygmalion", Bernard Shaw's professor declares he can take a flower girl of the slums and make her into a real lady. "Think like a duchess, act like a duchess, talk like a duchess - curbstone English keeps you in the gutter," he says to her. When you try to put such thoughts as these in your mind, if it is like the average mind, I can hear it reply, "Don't bother me. I haven't time for these things. I've got enough to think about now. I'll get along all right."

"What's that?" I can hear you answer, "You haven't time for these things?" "Nonsense. You've as much time as anybody. You'd better get Arnold Bennett's little book: "How to Live on Twenty-four Hours a Day." It will open up possibilities to you, and it costs less than a dollar. You'll get along all right, will you? Well, how about your study program? You haven't time to do any more studying? You mean the real truth is that you haven't time to do other things."

So the average mind answers back. Daring people can't afford not to think, just as you can't afford not to exercise. The big prizes are for those who dare to think hard, to think often, to think creatively. I've spent a lifetime in business, but never before have I seen such a demand for ideas. Ideas have always been the dynamos that move civilization forward. Stephenson had an idea of a locomotive long before rails were laid, but it took years and years before his idea was accepted. Today, ideas get an audience immediately. Industry is at the feet of creative thinkers begging for ideas.

Not many years ago a professor at Oberlin College suggested to his class that some day a new metal called aluminum would be economically produced so that it could be used for a thousand practical purposes. He said, "It has never been set free. A fortune awaits the man who can release aluminum." That word fell as seed into the mind of Charles Hall, a young boy less than twenty years of age. He was the son of a missionary to the West Indies. He began to work with little crucibles furnished by the professor and finally showed him a drop of pure aluminum and then dared to set out to discover aluminum in commercial quantities. He did, and when he died he left one-third of his immense aluminum fortune to Oberlin College, one-third to Foreign Missions. The other third he left to Berea College and the American Missionary Association. Oberlin gave an idea and a dare to Charles Hall, and he gave back to Oberlin a rich dividend. The whole world benefited when Charles Hall dared to think creatively along uncharted fields.

Most of the unexplored regions of the world may have been discovered, but what a field lies ahead for the mental Columbus, the thinking Peary, the planning Byrd. Physical adventure promises not half the thrill of mental adventure. Physical life brings happiness, but mental life brings interest - a consuming, absorbing interest. How I pity that person, young or old, who cannot shut out the world, open a book, and go forth on an adventure of romance, travel, biography, history or business. What a shame to see so many mental lives slow down after school days are over, just because people forget the necessity of everlastingly studying if they expect to get anywhere. Theodore Roosevelt died with a book under his pillow, consuming the ideas of others until the very last. Have you read Abbé Dimnet's "The Art of Thinking"? If not, buy it right away. Don't get it from the library. Own it. Lose no time. Its pages fascinatingly lead you into a new mental realm. If you already have a copy, dust it off and read it over again. Stagnant minds are the greatest obstacles to progress.

I spent an afternoon with Charles F. Kettering, President of the General Motors Research Corporation, and one of the keenest creative minds in America. After he moved to the city and "became famous", so the story goes, his mother still lived on the old home place in the country and burned coal-oil lamps. Why shouldn't she have bright lights just as he had in the city? He must see to it. He did. Result? The Delco system which illumined the farmhouses of our country. Mr. Kettering got tired of jumping out of his car and cranking it up. Why not start the car from a switch on the dashboard? Off went the creative mind on another excursion - the self-starter was the result. He found that it took 31 days to paint an auto, one coat on another with the proper time for drying. The paint men got their heads together, they thought that one day or possibly two at the outside might be saved. Kettering said he wanted it done in one hour. He was crazy! But a way was found. On some toys, a quick drying enamel was used. It wouldn't do for autos. Why? "It dries too damn fast." When he would spray it, he found that it would dry before it reached the surface. He kept on until Duco was produced and an auto was painted complete in an hour.

On one occasion Mr. Kettering brought a group of automobile manufacturers into a conference. He told them to write down all the improvements they would want for the next four years and leave their slips of paper on his desk. Then he took them through his research laboratory, showing them what was in progress. Coming back, one man reached for his paper and tore it up. "Hey, there, what do you mean?" said Mr. Kettering. "We only asked for little five-cent improvements. We didn't know how to ask for enough. You are years and years ahead of us," was the reply.

In St. Louis we had an outstanding brain surgeon who was head of our Washington University brain surgery clinic. His operations were almost miraculous. Cases were brought to him from thousands of miles away. "Lucky beggar", says the young medical student, "to be born with such skill." But wait a minute, let us look at Dr. Ernest Sachs' history.

A number of years ago, when he was an intern in a New York hospital, one of his chiefs bemoaned the fact that the majority of brain tumors were fatal. He prophesied that some day some surgeon would dare to find out how to save these lives. Young Ernest Sachs dared to be that surgeon. He dared to face an almost hopeless task. There was no background of successful brain surgery in America at that time. The only possible guidepost the young adventurer could steer for was a doctor in England, Sir Victor Horsley, who knew more about the anatomy of the brain than any other living man. He was the pioneer in brain surgery in England. Dr. Sachs received permission to study under this English scientist. But here is an interesting thing that he did before studying in England.

In order to become rooted and grounded in the knowledge and technique that he should possess before working under this eminent surgeon, he spent six months studying in Germany under the most able men there. Not many young students would be willing to do that. The English doctor was so impressed with the earnestness and industry of the young American who would spend six months in pre-preparation that he brought him right into his home. Together during two years they worked out long and intricate experiments on many dozens of monkeys. Thus the basic facts were found and the background laid for Dr. Sachs' future career.

He returned to America and here was laughed at when he asked for the opportunity to treat brain tumors. For years he fought discouragements and obstacles. He worked without facilities, but with that unconquerable urge that gets things done. Today the majority of brain tumors can be cured. Today Dr. Sachs shares his gifts by the training of young doctors and establishing them in different centers of this country so that each section may have a brain surgeon nearer home. His book, "The Diagnosis and Treatment of Brain Tumors" has been adopted the standard authority on this baffling subject.

Tong-g-g-g-g-g! A Serbian shepherd boy struck the handle of a long knife. The blade was buried in the ground of the pasture field so the signal did not reach the marauders hiding in the long corn nearby. But it did reach other shepherd boys scattered across the field, each with an ear pressed tight against the ground. By means of this ingenious system of sending signals through the ground the Serbian shepherd boys outwitted the Romanian cattle thieves who crept up under cover of darkness and the tall corn.

All except one of those shepherd boys grew up and forgot all about the phenomenon of the ground signals. But one boy remembered and twenty-five years later applied the principle with the result that he made one of the greatest inventions of the age. So Michael Pupin, that humble shepherd boy, changed the telephone from a device that could be used to speak only across a city to a long distance instrument that could be heard across a continent.

The Edisons and the Marconis were the long-range thinkers of yesterday. Wanted-some long-range thinkers today! Where yesterday a hundred new inventions were made, a thousand new ones will be made tomorrow and some of you who read this message will dare to make them. I read an article not long ago where somebody prophesied conditions twenty years from now. Our homes would be artificially cooled in the summer just as they are artificially heated in the winter. Transportation will be just as different from today as today is from the gay '90's. People will dress differently, think differently, live differently. Are you leaders going to sit back and wait for yourselves to be adapted to these conditions? Or, are you going to be one of those who help bring about these changes?

"I have no opportunity to create," you say. No opportunity? Bosh! Opportunities to create are popping out at you every minute of the day. Some of the greatest creations have come from minds able to interpret the usual in an unusual way.

Once a professor hit upon a great discovery while buttoning up his vest. Or rather, he hit upon the discovery because his vest wouldn't button up. His little daughter had sewn up some of the buttonholes. His fingers were going along as usual in their most intricate operations of buttoning a button. If you want to know how intricate these operations are, you might try it yourself. Just try consciously buttoning up one button. But be sure and count each thing that each thumb and finger does. Each move that they make. Then you will be able to start on this story where the professor started.

His buttoning was going on in the usual way, when something happened. A button wouldn't button.

The fingers fumbled helplessly for a moment, then sent out a call for help. The mind woke up. The eyes looked down . . . a new idea was born, or rather a new understanding of an old idea. What the professor had discovered was that fingers can remember. They call it physiological memory now.

Then he began playing pranks on his classes, and he found that the answer was always the same. As long as they could keep on doing the things they had always done, their minds wouldn't work. It was only when he figuratively sewed up their buttonholes, stole their notebooks, upset their routine, threatened them with failure, that any thinking was done.

So he came to the great, and now generally accepted, conclusion that the mind of man is "an emergency organ," that it relegates everything possible to other functions of the body as long as it is able, that it is only when the old order of things won't work any longer that it gets on the job.

I am indebted to an advertisement in the New York Times for the above on a man buttoning up his vest. But history is full of such commonplaces that turn our minds topsy-turvy.

One day in Denmark, Dr. Finsen stood gazing absent-mindedly out of his window. A cat lay dozing in the sun. The shadows lengthened and slowly shut off the sun from the cat. Tabby awoke, got up and went farther into the sun. Again the shadows crept up and again the cat moved into the sunlight. Finsen's curiosity was aroused. What made the cat stay in the sun? If light and heat are good for a cat, wouldn't they be good for people? And that was the starting point of his world-famous light-cure work.

Igo Etrich, the inventor of the Taube flying machine, got his idea in India from the seed of the zanonia. The turned-up wing tips of this natural "plane" became the principle of the war-famous German fighting plane.

Dr. Holmes, a noted psychologist, says that 95% of people think an aimless, desultory, gossipy flow of ideas and only 5% aim definitely direct, and definitely arrive at conclusions.

You daring adventurers in the mental realms - you can't all be Halls, Ketterings, Sachs, Pupins or Finsens, but you are not afraid to tackle the impossible, are you? "It can't be done" is a finality to those afraid to dare. But you crusaders are looking for things which can't be done. All the easy things have been done long ago. Now bring on the impossible!

Your mental program and the development of your mental self you must work out for yourself, but let me give you some of the few things that I have found very valuable in my own life. I am pretty much of the opinion that nobody was born a genius. I am coming more and more to Carlyle's definition of genius: "an infinite capacity for hard work." You have heard this over and over again, but have you benefited by it?

The other day one of our sales managers was talking about one of the brilliant young salesmen whom he employed a year before, who seemed to have the personality, the appearance and ability to go a long way. But he didn't, and the sales manager, after having fired him, told me that the man was just "plain dumb." He knew a little bit about everything, but when he got right down into a discussion of specific things, he just wasn't there. Only froth on top. I recall the flying fish I saw in the Indian Ocean. They flash up in the air for a minute, flutter and scintillate in the sun and then fall back into the sea. Who wants to be a flying fish, shining for a minute and then sinking out of sight? When it is so easy to get our thinking done for us, the big temptation is not to think. We glance at the newspaper headlines and let them form our opinions, and neglect to read the scholarly articles in the monthly magazine that would give us the meat on the subject. We listen to a few minutes of the radio and flatter ourselves that we know all about the Symphony. We read a review of a play and decide that we don't need to see the play itself. These are the temptations of the average person today, but if you have read this far, I assume that you are above the average person. I am daring you to know at least one thing well. What is it? Make your decision and then determine to know that one thing well, better than anyone else. In doing this you will have to think. No one is going to get far these days unless he thinks for himself. This is going to take time and hard work, but the joy you will discover in knowing one thing well will more than repay you.

I remember a story they used to tell about old Bill Brown down in my section of the country. He used to plow the field in the spring with a yoke of oxen. He would holler "Gee" and "Haw" at them, but they paid no attention to him. "Then go any way you durn please," said Bill, "the whole field has got to be plowed anyway." No crusader can turn his mental powers loose. Life has to be lived, the field has to be plowed, but it's the way you live it and the way you plow that count in the long run. You are alert. How dare you let mental oxen lead you around the field? You are the crusaders who are going to do things. You must plow a better furrow than ever has been plowed, even if it is only one furrow. You must harvest a better crop than ever has been harvested, even if it is only a few bushels. You recognize the danger as well as the disgrace of a half-used mind. You are going to gear up your mind to capacity and share its strength with others. Instead of diminishing by sharing, you will grow increasingly strong.

Train for the fight. Fit yourself for larger responsibility by studying outside of regular hours. Reading the right kinds of books improves your background and stimulates your brain. This minute, why not write down the name of one particular book you can't afford not to read? You know where you are headed. Then do some more exploring in that field through books. I'd like to recommend my rule of thumb for a minimum program: "I'll read one book a month." I use the last blank page of a book to make suggestive notes so that I can in the future catch at a glance the high points of the book which may be of personal profit to me.

You have to train for your mental crusade just as you train for your physical game of life. You can do that in the same time you spend on the comic page in the daily paper. It will benefit you a lot more.

I have always loved good books. Titles, as well as contents, start me on new adventures. The first book I can remember was called "Purpose." I don't know who wrote it. My mother gave it to me when I was a slip of a boy. Its very name went deep into my life. In later years I read "The Charm of the Impossible" by Margaret Slattery and "The Lure of the Labrador Wild" by Dillon Wallace - thrilling titles that stir the soul and make you want to do something. Then "One Increasing Purpose," "So Big," "Giants in the Earth," "The Quest of the Best," "He Can Who Thinks He Can," "Magnificent Obsession," "Men of Iron." How these titles gripped me. "The Psychology of Achievement" by Pitkin, and "The Marks of an Educated Man" by Wiggam, are among my favorites. Some critics may laugh at this, but somehow titles as well as contents seem to put a dare into me.

"He has the notebook habit," I heard a man say. Well, that's one of my mental habits which has proven very valuable in more ways than one. It is all right to develop your memory but I have found a notebook a most valuable memory aid. I always carry one in my inside coat pocket. I even keep one close beside my bed and many a time in the middle of the night I have jotted down something that I could never have recalled had I not had a pencil and paper handy.

Speaking of habits, how about some other old habit that is making a fool of you right before your eyes? The thing to do is to turn the whole procedure around and make a fool of that old habit. It is really a ridiculous situation that a mind of inherent strength cannot have its own way and master any habit.

One of our advertising men told me he had been smoking so many cigarettes the habit was making a fool of him, robbing him of his physical reserves. So, he decided to make a fool out of that habit. And here's the way he turned the tables:

He knew if he went around feeling sorry for himself because he couldn't smoke, he was sunk. It was all right to say "exert his will power," but that made his temper short and his work suffer. He decided the thing to do was to get a new habit immediately to replace smoking.

Now, he says, when we see him standing in front of an open window taking deep breaths, he is smoking. When he disinfects his throat with a gargle, he is smoking. When he is brushing his teeth directly after eating, he is smoking. In that way he formed new habits that have taken the place of the old smoking one.

John was a great dreamer. He built castles in the air a mile high - and left them in the air.

Bill was also a dreamer. He, too, built his air castles. But he had the faculty of bringing those castles down to earth. He would pile them in front of him. Then he would attack them and counter-attack them. He was as merciless in his cross- examination as any officer giving a criminal the third degree. Dreams that were wild he pulled out of the pile as he would pull a wet faggot out of the fire. But of those other dreams, the worthwhile ones, he demanded action. He ordered them to come true. Yes, Bill was a dreamer, but in addition he had that rare executive ability that tested, selected, then made his dreams come true.

Try Bill's methods. You have dreams. They will come true - I ask you when?

Most of us would like to be a Bernard Shaw or a Thomas A. Edison today. But how many would have been willing to be a Shaw or an Edison many years ago when they were constantly laboring, studying, training, and devouring all they could find which would fit them for the fame that was to be theirs? Ask your author friends if each book doesn't represent months, even years of hard labor. No man can give out unless he first takes in. You can't give what you don't have. Let me give you a challenge, a definite mental challenge. For one solid month, dare to think fearlessly in some one uncharted field. When you read a book don't let the author do all of your thinking for you. Stop at the end of that sentence, or page, or chapter which brings you up with a start. Interpret these thoughts into something definite in your own life. How can you apply it in your work tomorrow? Venture courageously into new mental realms. Think originally. If you can contribute one ounce of original thought, if you can originate just one new idea, you have dared well. This is to be your mental offensive campaign. Let's become sick and tired of being always on the defensive.

Finally, don't you dare stop until you have produced at least one creative idea. One creative mind dared to put the hind end of a needle on the point - a little thing, but out of it came the sewing machine. The Hindenburg line wasn't crossed easily. You'll have to adventure in No Man's Land and dig in many times before you reach your objective. The Allied Armies paid the price, but they smashed through. I dare you, I double dare you, to be a Creator - a Hunger Fighter, a Microbe Hunter. Make a start! Never stop until you can put down in black and white some one idea or thing that you have created.

May I add one word about the subconscious mind? As a business man, I don't know one thing about it, but I'm going to learn. If I can set my subconscious mind like an alarm clock before I go to bed at night, then wake up in the morning brimful of ideas, I'll keep in the Daring class. Better have a program to include the subconscious.

Perhaps what I have said here sounds too big and mighty to be accomplished. "I am not a genius. I haven't the capacity to be a Hunger Fighter, or a great scientist, or an author." Well, let's not think what you cannot do. What interests me is what you can do. Are you satisfied with what your mind has accomplished so far? Has it done the best it is capable of? I'll warrant it has not. Then your job is to know how much more mental ability you have, then dare to use it.

Remember that valuable possessions multiply when shared. Your mind begins to grow as you share it. How much more enjoyable is a book when you discuss it or maybe lend or pass it to friends with certain passages marked. You are a multiplier when you clip a good idea from the morning paper and pass it along to that person who is particularly interested. Telling an unusual story to others helps you fix it in your mind. How much more clearly a problem crystallizes in our mind when we present it to another. You give a big idea to your friend. He gives a big idea to you. You both have two ideas. Sharing increases.

Alas, there are some who will agree to all this and say, "That's good stuff," then never do a blessed thing. Or, they will try just one thing then another, but they will do them in a half-hearted way. They will never get anywhere. But you Crusaders, you are going to do these things. You are alert. You recognize the danger as well as the disgrace of a half-used mind. You are going to gear up your mind to capacity and share its strength with others. Instead of diminishing by sharing, you will grow increasingly strong.

Outline on a sheet of paper the following or a similar program for your Mental Dare. The weak ones who are licked or partially licked will stall here. Will you listen to the little imps whispering in your ears that writing down the things you ought to do is merely piffle? Or will you put things down in black and white that need to be done and never quit until you can say: "Done!"?

My Mental Dares	My Mental Accomplishments
1. One Habit to about-face	1. When conquered
2. One Idea to Create	2. Creative Development
3. One month's thinking in uncharted fields	3. Results obtained
4. My program is growing by sharing	4. What progress?
5. What is my biggest Mental Dare for the year ahead?	5. Daringly done

I DARE YOU TO DEVELOP A MAGNETIC PERSONALITY

If you were applying to us for a position in our business, I would first ask the doctor to report on your physical condition. I would want to be sure that you were well and had the stamina and strength to finish any program you would start. Then I would have the Personnel Department check your mental capacity and background. After being satisfied that you are physically and mentally fit, do you think that is all I want to know about you? Not by long odds. I want to see you and talk to you. But why? Isn't all the information we need to know on these reports? No, there is something more I must know, something that can't easily be put down on paper.

You walk into my office. I may notice the cut of your clothes, the way you comb your hair, your shoes, your nails, any stains on your fingers - we always give each other the "once over," don't we? But the big thing is, have you got that something called Personality. It may be akin to that "It" which I used to hear our young people talk about. I am looking for that indescribable quality which attracts people to you. If you give me a flabby handshake, if you have a grouchy look with the corners of your mouth turned down - we don't want you around. Faces that smile, voices that ring, steps that are firm, interests that are broad, likeable personalities. These are the things that attract business and the whole world, too, for that matter. Obstacles just melt away before the sunshine of a smile. Such leaders with the ability to make friends can dare twice as much as the lone wolf.

What is this Personality? Is it "That Something" born in some people and not in others? Can it be developed? Of course it can. Undoubtedly some people are blest with a greater capacity for this social side than others. Because Bill has more personality than I have doesn't mean that I shouldn't develop mine. Many a country boy has joined our sales force and been almost too timid to interview prospective consumers. But I have seen these same boys in a few years so develop and broaden their personalities that they now stand on a platform before hundreds of people and speak with confidence, poise, and power. These boys attract their audiences, not by memorizing their speeches, but by finding out a community's needs and with the fervor of an evangelist supplying those needs. Service is a much-overused word, but the development of real service is the enlargement of personality.

"But what am I to dare in the social side?" you ask. Shall I be a social lion? Not exactly. Perhaps your particular dare is not to be a social lion. If dancing, bridge and clubs take more than their share of time from the other three sides of your checker, I dare you to give them their proper place. Perhaps here is an idea that will help you develop that magnetic personality so essential to the complete life.

In the daily paper you read of some great man who has passed on. Who will dare to fill his shoes? Think of all the friends he has left behind, his influence in business and education. He has been an uplifting power in the community. Paying his bills and fulfilling his lawful obligations have been the smallest parts of his life. What was his personality? What particular things about him inspired his associates and drew people to him? Having discovered what the world has lost through the absence of this personality, why not dare to put it back into the living again? Live as that man lived. Think as he would think. Try to fill his place. As a young man I met John Wanamaker. His fine ideals and business ability deeply impressed me. Later when a problem came up that needed sound judgment, I would say, "How would John Wanamaker decide?" This program of trying to fill the shoes of a great man who has gone on may stagger you. You haven't the stuff in you to give. But you have something. Make a start. Give what you have. Every little bit that you give increases your personality by much more than you give.

Personality is a vague, intangible thing to talk about on paper. But how real, how tremendous it is in life all around us! I like the way Miss Helen Gill Lovett described personality. During her active teaching years, she was on our American Youth Foundation Summer Camp Staff and used the different sources of water at the Camps to illustrate four different kinds of personality.

The first is like a mountain stream at the New Hampshire Camp. It sings as it tumbles down the hills into the lake and wherever we touch it there is a supply of fresh pure water. Some personalities are like that. Whether you meet them on the mountaintop or down at the lake, they are always sparkling, always singing. Their presence chases gloom and inspires us to go joyfully along with them. Where they lead, all follow; when they smile, all smile; and they are always ready to stimulate us and quench our thirst by sharing with us all they have.

P. G. Orwig, the long-time Director of the American Youth Foundation, is a mountain stream personality. His Indian name is "Wadjepi," the nimble one. If you meet him in camp or on a duck hunt or on the street, or in his home, I dare you to go away depressed. "Wadjepi" gives everybody he meets a refreshing smile, an infectious laugh, a mental pat on the back. He wasn't born with all this capacity. He developed it by giving it away. When he sees someone with the "blues" he turns on the sunshine. I like to be around "Wadjepi."

Down by the lake into which the mountain stream tumbles is a spring. It illustrates the second kind of personality. It is more quiet than the singing mountain stream, but from its bubbling depths comes the coldest, most refreshing drink. The depth and strength of many quiet lives are a joy and blessing when shared with others.

"Dad" Waite, former associate director with P. G. Orwig in the American Youth Foundation, is the deep spring personality. He is a comforter, a helper. "Dad" expresses his personality because to thousands he is a father, sympathetic, helpful and understanding.

In the Michigan Camp there was an old pump that squeaked terribly when it worked. But if you had patience and endurance enough to keep pumping it brought up pure cold water from a deep well. A few years ago I was eating breakfast on a French diner on the way to Marseilles where I was to take sail for India. An Englishman came in and sat opposite me. He ordered tea. He was plainly unsociable. The French waiters were slow bringing his tea, and his ire kept rising. Finally they brought him a cup of coffee. He drank it without sugar or cream, growling all the time that he had ordered tea. They brought him a second cup of coffee. By that time he was ready to explode, but he drank it and proceeded to tell all French waiters what would happen if he did not get his tea. If I had left the diner at that time I would have gone away with the conviction that he was a very disagreeable person. But, fortunately, his tea arrived and with it his good humor. He introduced himself to me, discovered we were to be on the same boat going to India, and later on was the means of making scores of contacts for me in the Far East that were unexpected and by far the most interesting part of my visit there. More than that, we struck up a lasting friendship and I have discovered him to be one of the most interesting personalities I know. Don't always judge a pump by the squeaks it makes, nor a chance acquaintance. Keep on drawing out to find the deeper treasure of rich personality down the well. And vice versa remember that to be cranky and ill-tempered may be over-shadowing your good qualities to such an extent that you are driving friends away from you. The job of your personality is to attract, not to repel.

Close beside the pump site is a Memorial Fountain. Built of boulders, strong and imposing, it makes a striking appearance. It is connected to an abundant water supply and through it four bubbling fountains bring cold water to the thirsty. But this past summer there was a new patent connection with the sources of supply and this connection got out of order. The fountain above was beautiful. The water below was pure and bountiful, but just a little something wrong and the fountain was of no practical use. Personality is an illusive thing. Good looks, good habits, good education, fine family, magnificent supply of the best of life to draw from, and yet something lacking in the connections.

I know a girl like that fountain. She had so much to give, but never gave. At present she is a woman soured on life, blaming everybody but herself for her melancholy. In reality, it is her own selfishness to blame. She allowed her personality to get "out-of-order" and she never fixed it.

If you are as I am you will want a few rules that you can get your teeth into. "All of this talk about personality is all right," I can hear you saying, "but what can I do specifically to develop my personality?" The only way I can answer this is from my own practical experience. The first thing that I would do to develop my social side would be to make worthwhile contacts.

When I was a young man, Henry M. Flagler's name was on every tongue. He was treasurer of the Standard Oil Company and a close associate of John D. Rockefeller. Mr. Flagler poured his riches into Florida, building the East Coast Railroad across the Florida Keys and also a chain of hotels. At one time I was in Palm Beach when he was just completing a marble palace for his home. I determined to meet Mr. Flagler. I felt that the inspiration of such a successful man would have a stimulating effect on my whole life. It was easy for me to meet people on my own level, but how was I ever going to meet such a big man as Mr. Flagler? If I didn't meet people who thought bigger, acted bigger and were bigger - much bigger than myself I argued, how could I ever grow bigger? Here I was in the same town with a man who had become one of the most outstanding successes in America. I had no pull, no introductions, but "fools rush in where angels fear to tread." So I wrote him a frank note telling him that I was a young man full of ambition, just starting in business and that I had a great desire to meet him. To my immense surprise an answer quickly came back inviting me to his home. I feel embarrassed, even now, to think how long I stayed. That day is a highlight in my memory. He showed me his home. I never was in such fairyland before, never knew such splendor existed. We walked around his beautiful gardens. He told me of Mr. Rockefeller and those early beginnings with mountainous obstacles. My mind was filled to saturation. At one time, I remember stopping short and saying, "Mr. Flagler, this is a great privilege to me. Your experiences thrill me. I'm afraid I will forget some of the rules of your life. Do you mind if I write them down in my notebook?" (Even then I had a little book with me and had started the habit of making notes.) "Certainly not," said Mr. Flagler. Then I wrote "Great Responsibility-Great Accountability," and page after page of his rules of life. I feel a glow even now as I think over that rare interview.

The day after I met Mr. Flagler it was impossible for me to act on the same plane as I had acted the day before. Incidentally, that taught me a very vivid lesson: a man who has made a success has a responsibility to those who are striving to make a success. I would like to believe also that the time he gave me in recalling memories helped him to pass along the finer things for which his life stood.

That day with Mr. Flagler was a turning point in my life. That chance meeting with the man in the French dining car made my trip to India a rare experience instead of just an ordinary tour. I try to learn something from every great personality with whom I come into contact. If I don't learn something from him I am to blame and I have wasted the time of the greater personality.

For instance, after meeting Ozora S. Davis, formerly of the Chicago Theological Seminary, I said to myself, "What is that rich inspiring something in this man's personality? How can I acquire it so I can inspire others as he has me?" From Sherwood Eddy I have always tried to capture that urge which sends him around the world for a cause - that "something more" which stirs men to high achievement. When I meet Charles R. Brown I try to absorb some of his magnetic spark so that I, too, might quicken the souls of men around me. And from Dr. Joel E. Goldthwait I try to catch his secret of inspiring men and women to take proper care of their physical selves so as to live gloriously. Yes, I have found it pays to come into contact with great men, but it pays more to try to emulate them.

I read in the New York Journal a fable which illustrates one of the best personality rules which I could give you to develop contacts of all kinds.

"The North Wind and the Sun disputed which was the most powerful, and agreed that he should be declared the victor who could first strip a way-faring man of his clothes.

"The North Wind first tried his power, and blew with all his might, but the keener became his blasts, the closer the traveler wrapped his cloak around him, till at last, resigning all hope of victory, he called upon the Sun to see what he could do.

"The Sun suddenly shone out with all his warmth. The traveler no sooner felt his genial rays than he took off one garment after another, and at last, fairly overcome with heat, undressed, and bathed in a stream that lay in his path.

"Persuasion is better than force."

I dare you to develop that magnetic personality that will lead and inspire others. You can have that personality if you have a great enough desire. You can become pretty much what you want to be. Can you imagine a young man with a sincere and earnest desire to make friends, ever turning out a grouch? If a young woman really desires to be an interesting conversationalist, she will be one.

When I was a young man I saw the advertisement of a book guaranteeing to develop personal magnetism. It cost me three dollars and I didn't have any three dollars to squander. The book said, "When you enter a room everybody will say, 'Look, there he comes.' " I hadn't read very many pages until I realized that personality is developed from within and that a book only gives you suggestions to work out for yourself. I did get one or two valuable helps which have stayed with me and which I'm going to pass on to you. "Always walk on the sunny side of the street. The warmth and power of the sun enter your system. Its rays give your face a glow and you reflect sunshine to others." With that conscious thought in my mind, I still walk on the sunny side of the street. Then again, "When you wash, put your head down in the basin, and always wash your face up, not down. Wash the corners of your mouth up into a smile and not down into a grouch." Of course, personality depends on more than such superficial things. But the big thought I got out of it all was, if the desire to be sunny and smiling and interesting was strong enough, then every action such as walking and washing influenced our personality.

What are the ways to develop personality? They are simple things and easily overlooked, but they are very vital in the building of this side of a complete life. In looking back over the men of great personality I have known and do know there are certain common characteristics they all have. For instance, Mr. Flagler had a broad sympathy. He was able to put himself in my shoes. He was able to understand a young man, ambitious, wanting to get ahead. That taught me a lesson - that in developing personality one must develop broad sympathies toward everyone no matter from what station in life he comes.

Another thing I noticed in great personalities with whom I have come into contact is that they always develop a characteristic of leadership. Not only in big things but in little things. For instance, I have noticed if I meet a really big man and walk only a few blocks with him he gives me something stimulating to think about. It may be one of his own problems or one of my problems or the question of how to help put over the Community Fund this year, or next month's business program, or any kind of program - but he has led my mind and me into a new realm. It's a pretty good rule to remember that every time we come into contact with another person, even though just walking a block, our job is to lead him to a higher plane than that one on which we found him.

The other day a young friend of mine called and congratulated me on my wedding anniversary. When he went out of his way to do this little courtesy, it reminded me of another quality which great personalities have - that of thoughtfulness. Incidentally, this young man is rapidly developing a fine personality. I reflected that this quality of thoughtfulness for others was one of the reasons why. We cannot go on a glorious crusade and forget the fellow crusader who is marching at our elbows. We cannot develop personality if we entirely ignore the man at the desk across from us. In thinking of the big things of life don't overlook the little things because this quality of thoughtfulness is mainly concerned with little things. I have always found a notebook has been my best help to develop this trait of thoughtfulness. Record birthdays, anniversaries, children's names, interesting events. When you make a new contact it doesn't take long to write a note showing that you appreciated it. It isn't any gift you send, it's the thought that goes with it that endears you to others. Thoughtfulness is a giving of yourself. It's easy to pick up a telephone and wish your associate in business Godspeed on the journey he is undertaking. That doesn't take much of your time, but how it increases the zest with which he undertakes that journey. You only have to leave for the office five minutes earlier to drop by the hospital to see that acquaintance who is ill. Ten minutes tonight, before you eat your dinner, spent in writing a longhand note to your very gracious host of the other night will cement a friendship that will mean much to you and to the host. A millionaire in money is nothing compared to being a millionaire in friends, and everyone can be this, provided you keep these friends when you make them. And thoughtfulness in little things is the best way I know to keep them.

There are many more qualities which one can use to develop personality. These are just some of the outstanding ones. You yourself must have learned the things that build up this social side of your life. There is one other, however, before we close this chapter, which I believe will prove very valuable in your life. That is to treat everybody alike, no matter from what station in life he comes. Be your own self with all people whether they be prince or pauper. This may sound like a bromide, but look around you at the people you know. Unfortunately, there are many people in the world so constituted that they are always licking the boots of those over them and lording it over those under them. That's a sure way to destroy personality. On the other hand, really great men and women are those who are natural, frank and honest with everyone with whom they come into contact.

For a long time I have been going to the Gulf Coast each winter to shoot ducks. In the blinds you spend a lot of time thinking and waiting. Often I find myself wondering what it is in the fall that starts these wild ducks and other migratory birds on their long journey from the Hudson Bay in the Northland clear down to the Gulf Coast and even farther; and then in the spring, what starts them back North again. Is it some inner urge that whispers timidly at first as the leaves begin to turn? And then does it grow and grow with the wintry blasts into an overwhelming obsession until it governs every action of the bird and finally sends it on its long migration across the continent? Or is it only in the restless breast of the leader that the urge to go becomes an all-consuming one? Is he the one that persuades the others that now is the time to get up and go? At any rate, something happens to all Duckland. Something so urgent and so irresistible that not a single duck can disregard it. Old ducks, young ducks, weak ducks, strong ducks - they all go and fly as far as they have strength toward their destination because of some daring urge within them.

That's the kind of urge you must possess. Something so overwhelming that you can't resist it. A "Magnificent Obsession" that wakes you in the morning with a desire to serve that cannot be put aside. Something that sends you into any group, not with the thought, "what can I get out of them," but rather with "what can I give."

It is this social side of life where our principle that valuable possessions when shared multiply becomes doubly effective. Here truly. the more you give the more you are capable of giving. I dare you to develop the fine art of finding, making, and keeping friends by genuine giving of your time and personality to others. Look for the best in people. Learn to like people. Find out what they are interested in. Select five new people this month. Show yourself friendly to each one by giving him some particular little courtesy. Then watch what happens. At the end of the month, you have five new friends, and inside a deeper capacity for friendship and a richer personality.

You can be bigger socially than you have ever been in your life. That's sure. In the social realm results are immediately evident because every day you are reacting on others. You can't grow socially unless you help others grow also. My social Dares are so simple, right down to earth.

I dare you, Winning Smile, to replace Old Man Grouch.

I dare you, Mr. Snapping Turtle, to depart to another climate.

I dare you, Flabby Fingers, to develop into a Warm Handclasp.

I dare you, my own Personality, to become a Welcome Guest everywhere.

I dare you, my Social Self, to generate that Magnetic Spark which leads to a charmed life.

To accomplish these Dares and possess that intangible something which attracts people, I would suggest definite consideration of the following questions, which should be written down on a sheet of paper and stuck in your mirror. When you have answers that show definite progress, add those to the sheet.

1. Am I a greater or lesser factor in my community than I was a year or two years ago?

1. What is my program?

2. Was there ever a time in my life when I was contributing more to the welfare of others than I am now'?

2. What are my aggressive plans?

3. Is the level of my frlendship up from a year ago up -or down?

3. How to make more and better friends plans.

4. Are jealousy, grouchiness, bad temper, or any other social handicaps increasing or decreaslng in my life?

4. My plans for stamping them out.

5. Is it possible to picture any other environment under which I would increase my accomplishments?

5. What is this improved environment?

6. What's My Big Social Dare?

6. When shall it be Daringly Done?

7. Dare I dare to become like some great outstanding personality?

7. Progress.

I DARE YOU TO BUILD CHARACTER

We were climbing up the great trail toward the mountain peak. Jimmy, our five-year-old grandson, was struggling to keep up.

"Tired, Jimmy?" I asked.

"My feet are tired but myself isn't," he answered.

"Myself" was Jimmy's spirit. Up the Great Trail was an adventure for five-year-old Jimmy. Up the Great Trail will be an adventure for twenty-year-old Jimmy - yes, for thirty-year-old Jimmy and fifty-year-old Jimmy. As long as the spirit is there, Jimmy will continue to climb. Tired? Yes, of course, he will become tired. Yes, of course, body will be tired, but Jimmy's spirit never tires of urging him to higher and higher plateaus.

There is an old Hindu legend, says Claude Bragdon, that at one time all men on earth were gods, but that men so sinned and abused the Divine that Brahma, the god of all gods, decided that the godhead should be taken away from man and hid some place where he would never again find it to abuse it. "We will bury it deep in the earth," said the other gods. "No," said Brahma, "because man will dig down in the earth and find it." "Then we will sink it in the deepest ocean," they said. "No," said Brahma, "because man will learn to dive and find it there, too." "We will hide it on the highest mountain," they said. "No," said Brahma, because man will some day climb every mountain on the earth and again capture the godhead." "Then we do not know where to hide it where he cannot find it," said the lesser gods. "I will tell you," said Brahma, "hide it down in man himself. He will never think to look there."

And that is what they did. Hidden down in every man is some of the divine. Ever since then he has gone over the earth digging, diving and climbing, looking for that godlike quality which is hidden down within himself.

It is this spark that I am daring you to turn into a blaze. It is this radiance we must recapture. It is something genuine, something for everyday use. It is the spirit that naturally makes you do the right thing at the right time.

It's the thing that makes a gentleman and a gentlewoman. It is that unseen something that will not let you take advantage of a weaker person, whether it be on the football field or in a business transaction. It is that something inside of every worthwhile person that makes him decide right when temptation confronts him, be fair, be honest, and be dependable. And this spirit I am talking about is not one that skulks back in the shadows. It is one that belongs up with the captains and kings. It is a spirit proud of its heritage, one that flies its banner high.

Too much has been left to the preachers in the past. The day has gone when the radiant side of life can be located like a Sunday suit and only put on one day a week. I am still speaking to you as a practical businessman, daring you to live a complete life. What General would attack on three fronts and retreat on the fourth? Would you be fair to yourself to quit with three-fourths victory when complete victory is in sight? During the summer I sat high up on the sand dunes of our American Youth Foundation Camp in Michigan and watched the ever-changing glory of Lake Michigan by day and night. Sunrises and sunsets. Moon and stars. Water and sky that were never the same. But the thing that gripped me most was the horizon line. Some days it would be miles and miles away. On other days a mist would turn into a fog, and my horizon was just a stone's throw away. Who wants to live in a fog and be limited in his outreach? I know of no other side of life that will so widen your whole horizon as the development of this last and most important frontier.

It is to you, strong of body, brilliant of mind, magnetic in personality, that I am talking now. What price all of these without the inspiration of a Cause? Since the beginning of things, man has had the capacity for some kind of spiritual life. Unless this side is developed, it dies, and all the other three sides of life suffer. No man can allow part of himself to die without penalizing

45

the parts of him which continue to live. If attack is the keynote of growth in our physical, mental, and social lives, why not in the spiritual life, too?

I remember a dear old lady whose life was a constant benediction. Like an avenging angel she suddenly stood over them, silencing their chatter with words that pierced like swords. "How dare you criticize my Lord!" she demanded. And they all wondered how they had dared. You couldn't criticize General Washington with Anthony Wayne in the room. Who would dare say anything about Pasteur with any of his co-workers standing by? Why should any Spiritual Crusader sit passive when the Crusader of Galilee will take us on an adventure far beyond our fondest dreams?

Strength and courage are essential in the development of the physical, mental, and social sides of life. Aren't you willing to admit that you need these qualities on your spiritual front as well? Look at the Honor Roll of Crusaders. Are there any weaklings there? Saul of Tarsus persecuted the Christians until a light from heaven changed his whole life and he became Paul, the preacher, who stormed the very gates of Rome under the shadow of Death itself, to carry his Master's message to the needy. Was there any lack of adventure in his life? Peter, fiery and impetuous, was unwilling for Jesus to wash his feet. In his human weakness, he denied his Lord thrice. That same Peter, who caught the passion of service, was crucified head downwards. Whoever fought against greater odds to more far-reaching victories than those Spiritual Crusaders of old!

"What is a spiritual adventure?" you ask.

Here is a striking example. In St. Paul's Cathedral, London, on a tablet to the memory of General Charles Gordon-"Chinese Gordon"-I read these immortal words:
"Who at all times and everywhere gave
His Strength to the Weak
His Substance to the Poor
His Sympathy to the Suffering
His Heart to God."

Sir Wilfred Grenfell found, too, that all spiritual adventure had for its foundation first the giving of one's loyalty to a living leader and then expressing it in knightly service. "Real religion involves real courage," he writes. "The inefficiency which I had associated with it had not been its fault, but ours."

I am not asking you to become preachers like Paul or Peter, or a soldier like Gordon, or a medical missionary like Grenfell, but I am asking you to consider their revolutionary idea of making an adventure out of their religion. These men, with thoughts so like our very own, first fell into the false notion that religion was something for young children or old people, or for the weak or sickly, or the fanatics. But how different when they found that it was a power that worked in every phase of their own lives, building the physical, developing the mental, inspiring the social.

Maybe Sir Wilfred Grenfell's method of attack on the spiritual front will help us. Real religion dreams and sees visions that intoxicate every bit as much as the license permitted by the will not to believe. Only it intoxicates with deeds of kindness, justice, chivalry, love. It answers the insatiate demands of youth and high spirit for freedom from boredom and the pettiness of daily routine every whit as naturally and undeniably as dram-drinking, petting parties, gaming tables, or the self-pollution of lust and license which surely, if slowly, evoke the loathsome Hyde out of the knightly Jekyll which is in us. . .

This is from a man who saw life as a whole. In Labrador he became the great healer and the great lover of men. He made new men as well as new legs. He made the morally lame, as well as the physically lame, walk straight once more.

Doing right can be made actually more thrilling than doing wrong. Our Labrador hero has proven this by his daring deeds. The lure of the Labrador Wild was his spiritual adventure. You who risk the remorse of tomorrow for tonight's thrill, why not try the Grenfell kind of thrill that brings joy instead of remorse?

Lift your thoughts above the commonplace. Think on noble things. Soon you are on a higher level. If you consider religion something to be put up with, it becomes a drudgery. Exercise and study are a drudgery to one in the wrong mental attitude. But if you consider the building of character, or ethics, or morals, or religion- whatever you choose to call it - as an opportunity to grow, then the unseen things of life take on a new significance. My inspiring friend, Dr. Charles R. Brown, Dean Emeritus of Yale Theological Seminary, told my co-workers at our mill that he judges a man by his wants. If you don't want to be a spiritual adventurer, you never will. But if you sear into your brain and heart and soul a hunger for the best of life, a craving to grow, a cause for your crusade, then you have already advanced on the fourth front.

Dare to live in the Presence of the Best. Try for one week to live a distinguished life, surrounding yourself with the very best the world has to offer. Read an excellent poem. Begin the biography of a distinguished man. Study a painting by an Old Master. Hear a best Victrola record. Listen to a classical radio program or a symphony. See an uplifting play or movie. Hear a stirring speaker. Meet an inspiring personality. See a sunrise and a sunset. Strive to crowd out of your life unworthy thoughts, unworthy acts, unworthy contacts. Just see what will happen if, for a solid week, you fill your life only with the best! The very best in literature, the very best in art, the very best in nature. If only we would surround ourselves with the world's excellence, we would live like Kings!

Physical strength demands exercise. Mental alertness demands study. Winsome personality thrives on service. Religious growth requires action, the actual doing of right things instead of the wrong. We advance only by doing.

Say your prayers tonight, but unless tomorrow you can act on them, they are not worth much. Dr. E. Stanley Jones in his book, tells the following story:

"I once came down from Almore over one of the worst winding roads of the world. The driver of the bus had never driven in the Himalayas before, and it happened that on his first trip the previous day he had almost gone over one of those terrifying, precipitous cliffs. He was nervous; so before starting back he came in front of the engine and stood with folded hands, saying his prayers to the machine. That done, we started off, but had not gone far when the engine began to overheat. There was no water in the radiator! This was remedied. But when we were still many miles from our destination, the machine stopped while going up a hill. There was no petrol in the tank! There we stayed until rescued. The driver said his prayers to the machine, but put no water in the radiator and no petrol in the tank."

Why not start an offensive today? Couldn't you begin by putting your prayers into action? What definite right things will you do to replace some of the wrong things you have been doing? What particular hill will you take? Will you set a zero hour to go over some top that has stood as an obstacle in your life? List some of these things, and opposite them launch an offensive program. Imagine yourself a Paul or a Peter, or a Gordon, or a Grenfell, or that quiet friend of yours who is like the still waters that run deep, but whose life overflows with good deeds which bring rewards beyond measure. Better still, make a program that will be satisfied with nothing less than your own self at your very best all the time.

A thrilling spiritual adventure awaits you but it will take courage. The men who dared were the first pioneers to cross the wilderness. They were the front line men in the Great War. Courage challenged their inner resources. You cannot climb your spiritual heights without that same courage to loosen the powers that are within you.

Don't be discouraged if you fail in your first efforts. Coach Meehan of New York University says, "We learn practically nothing from a victory. All our information comes from a defeat. A winner forgets most of his mistakes."

It is not for me to tell you what your Spiritual Dare should be. You know your own life. There is just one big thing I dare you to do - Beat Your Best. Spiritual investments are repaid a thousand-fold. Don't worry about your few little loaves. Invest what you have. The returns will be far more than you realize. Catch some great challenge of service. Men do great deeds under a "Magnificent Obsession."

If you will write out the following questions and answer them carefully, it will help clarify your spiritual dares.

1. I have read Fosdick's "Twelve Tests of Character" and will grade myself.

2. Am I above or below the average on moral courage?

3. How dependable am I? How honest?

4. Was God ever more real to me than He is today?

5. My spiritual self is my greatest possession. Plan for its growth. What am I going to do to develop it this year? What crusade am I going to send it on next year?

6. What is my great Spiritual Dare?

7. Have I a great Cause in Life? A Magnificent Obsession?

Record your progress by writing the following questions on a sheet of paper. Then Dare to grade yourself. You will not want to stop until you have lifted yourself to your highest levels of satisfaction.

1. Twelve Tests Tested. Grade after three months.

2. What one thing have I done to improve my moral courage?

3. How have I dared to improve my dependability?

   My honesty?

4. What is my definite program for growth?

5. In what way have I shown spiritual growth during the past three months?

6. What have I done toward accomplishing my spiritual Dare?

7. Is my Cause any nearer accomplishment than it was three months ago?

I DARE YOU TO SHARE

Many of you have read Lloyd C. Douglas' "Magnificent Obsession." The plot is most unique and reveals in a most interesting way how a young man, with all the graces that one could desire, learned the secret of real social growth. He was rich and lived a spoiled, useless life, when an accident brought him up with a jolt. He recovered consciousness in a hospital to find he had been almost drowned. His life had been saved, however, by means of a pulmotor rushed over from the summer cottage of a world-famous brain surgeon. The unfortunate tragedy was that the surgeon was drowned while the pulmotor which could have saved his life was being used to save the ne'er-do-well. The story tells how the young man, realizing he had been indirectly responsible for the loss to the world of a great man, resolved to fill this great man's place by becoming an equally capable brain surgeon. That resolution became his Obsession, and eventually he accomplished his aim. But in so doing he discovered his "Magnificent Obsession." He found he must become more than a brain surgeon to fill the eminent man's shoes. The famous doctor had been an even greater personality in an entirely different sphere of life. Literally thousands of people had been helped in various ways by him. To some he had given money, to others his time, to others his skill. But always on one condition, that they should never during his lifetime reveal the fact of his help. His Theory had been that in giving of his possessions to others, unknown to the world, he was contributing to his own personality - that unheralded good deeds enlarged and enriched life. The story goes on to tell how the young man, filled with this "Magnificent Obsession," practiced the same theory and marched on to the same reward.

I would hate to think something tragic would be necessary to put a Magnificent Obsession into your life. The young man in the story found his urge when he discovered his aimless life had been saved at the expense of a worthy one. Then he dared to give back to the world what he had caused the world to lose. You are enjoying something today because of others' sacrifices. Doesn't that dare you to make good?

If one is to share properly he cannot shirk the responsibility of service. Community Funds, Red Cross drives have to be done by someone. Years ago when I was down in the Bahama Islands I found a red bean which the natives believed was the omen of good luck. I have carried those beans with me for many, many years and with them I founded what I like to call "The Good Turn Bean Society of the World." When one does me a really good turn I give him one of these red beans and make him a member of the Society. You would be surprised how many quarts of these beans I have sent for to replenish my supply. It just seems the whole world is made up of people who do good turns. Unless we want to be parasites we must do more good turns than others do to us. Because we are leaders and crusaders we are daring to attempt more than the other fellow. What time and thought and energy are we giving to community needs, to welfare work? All of these services must be done by someone not for pay. Pay comes in rich full measure by sharing.

"We Florentines," says one of George Eliot's characters, "live scrupulously that we may spend splendidly."

Another illustration I believe expresses this idea of sharing with others is the one used by Dr. Fosdick in "The Meaning of Service."

"The Sea of Galilee and the Dead Sea are of the same water. It flows down, clear and cool, from the Hermon and the roots of the cedars of Lebanon. The Sea of Galilee makes beauty of it, for the Sea of Galilee has an outlet. It gets to give. It gathers in its riches that it may pour them out again to fertilize the Jordan plain. But the Dead Sea, with the same water, makes horror. For the Dead Sea has no outlet. It gets to keep. That is the radical difference between selfish and unselfish men. We all do want life's enriching blessings - we ought to; they are divine benedictions. But some men get to give, and they are like Galilee, while some men get to keep and they are like the brackish water that covers Sodom and Gomorrah."

Let me tell you two true stories of sharing. One about the Richest Little Rich Girl I ever knew and the other about the Richest Little Poor Girl that I ever knew.

Mary Brendon's father was a rich steel manufacturer in the East. Of course, Mary Brendon isn't her real name. If I told you exactly who she was, she would scalp me. She had everything in the world she wanted - money, clothes, luxuries, everything. The World War came. She was determined to go to France. Her father was equally determined that she shouldn't. She won. Fathers have a great way of backing down, but not too graciously. She was accepted by the Y.M.C.A. With her violin (for she was an accomplished musician) she was off for overseas. I had charge of the Y work in the old Third Division, a unit of the regular army under Major General Joseph F. Dickman. We were in training at Chateau Villain. We had the best group of Y.M.C. A. workers in France. I acknowledge that. But we didn't have nearly enough. At the Y headquarters in Paris I was considered hard-boiled. Any weak or just ordinary, mediocre workers they would send down, I'd fire right back. You see, I was too old to enlist, had been a business man all my life, with experience in picking men, and I got into the Y because I wanted to do my share. Anyway, a bit of fighting and adventure were always to my liking. But one day Mary Brendon arrived with her violin under her arm. She brought a note from my friend, Helen King, who assigned all the girls, saying that she would stick. Mary looked as if a strong puff of wind would blow her away, but there she stood, clinging to her violin. There were no easy jobs. She was placed with the old Seventh Infantry. I get a shudder up my back now as I think of the work those girls did. They scrubbed their canteens, made literally barrels of hot chocolate, washed endless dishes. I'll bet Mary never washed a dish in all her life before. At night the men were entertained - and scant entertainment it was, too. Mary was everywhere, always with her violin, striking up a tune. How her boys could sing, and how they adored her! And well they might for the way she fought for supplies for her men. She would get so insistent at times that I wanted to send her back to Paris, but she had handled her father at home, and in her quiet way had learned to get what she wanted.

Our great day came. We were ordered to the front. Mary wouldn't be left behind. She followed her men right up to the Marne. The day before we were ordered into the lines for our first baptism of fire, our chaplains, Protestants and Catholics, planned communion for our men. There weren't chaplains enough to be everywhere. I pressed all our Y preachers into service. Poor little Mary was out of luck. She loved her men. She knew many of them would never come back, but we couldn't find a chaplain or minister for her anywhere so she must go without communion. But not so, Mary. "Please help me, Mr. Danforth," she pleaded. "I'll get the bread and wine and I'll play a hymn on my violin, and we will serve our men ourselves." And she did, bless her heart! Never in my life has a communion made such an impression on me.

July fifteenth and sixteenth, 1918, were awful days for the old Third Division. The Germans were driven back over the Marne, but our losses were terrific. Y trucks were turned into ambulances. Y men did heroic work. Never did our Y girls falter. Pressed into service at the dressing stations, Mary Brendon and the other girls cared for the wounded without batting an eye. Major General Dickman recognized such service on behalf of the Third Division Y with a beautiful citation. I could tell you a lot more about this Rich Little Rich Girl, but you know enough to catch the spiritual uplift of such a life.

Rich, talented, hard-working, courageous - yes, all of these. But she gave something more. It was Mary's spirit that lived in the hearts of all with whom she worked. She had offered her life in the service of her country and her God. She was working for a Cause, an all-consuming passion service absorbed her. And in her sharing what she had with others a richer life came back to her.

It is this same kind of Cause, a similar urge and a similar sharing, that I dare you to put into

50

your heart and soul.

Now let me tell you about my Rich Little Poor Girl. I'll name her Ruth Adams. Of course, that isn't her name. If she ever reads this, even without her name, she will protest to the heavens that there isn't a word of truth in my story. But by so doing she would be running true to form. To be strictly truthful, Ruth was neither rich nor poor. Her father was a professional man, and she was a strong and happy daughter, full of ideas which could not all be worked out in New England. The Great War was Over. The Near East Relief was caring for orphans and refugees in that hotbed of racial strife - Turkey, Armenia and Greece. The need was great. Self-sacrificing workers were few. Ruth Adams had been in the Near East before. She knew there was dirt and rags and typhus at the other end. Long hours, sickness, death - some never came back! No glamour of war. Nothing heroic about it - just a dirty, complicated job of trying to save children while politics and war broke down homes and killed off families who had every right to live. An inner urge possessed Ruth Adams. My, how it gets you. She would go!

I visited the Barracks in Constantinople. The sight of the refugees pouring in beggars description. Those who survived, weary and weak after their long trek, fell across the threshold. They were huddled into over-crowded, ill-ventilated rooms. The next morning those who died during the night were laid in piles like cordwood and carted away. The sight was worse than war, and I know war. Helpless women and children, hope gone, strength gone dying like rats - such scenes wrung our hearts. Here Ruth Adams worked. A barracks in her charge was ordered evacuated. Turkish soldiers cleared the building and reported that no one was left. Ruth didn't believe them. She would see for herself. On the top floor she found two women and a little child, who looked like a four or five-year-old, but who turned out to be eight years old. She demanded that they be removed. "No use; let they will die before morning and we'll cart them away. Save handling twice." That was the soldiers' reply. Roused to special effort because of the injustice and neglect of these refugees, Ruth Adams gave all the strength she possessed, and with only a driver's help, carried the women from the top floor to the car. Then she returned and in her own arms brought that little unconscious bundle of a girl down herself. She rushed them to the American Hospital in Stamboul. Hoping against hope, she laid the little child on a hospital bed and begged the nurses, as a final gesture, to pretend that the child had a chance to survive. She persuaded them to bathe and feed her as a convalescent who needs personal care for recovery, even though they knew all too well that they had little more than a corpse. Ruth left the hospital, rushing back to her work, knowing that her friends, the nurses, would do their utmost. They did and the child is alive today, miraculously saved.

Within a week Ruth Adams was brought into the same hospital. The dreaded typhus had caught her. She fought through weeks of unconsciousness, with expert care of doctors and nurses. Her indomitable spirit, together with their skill and a merciful Providence, pulled her through. I met her at the Mission when she was convalescing. Her pale cheeks told of her struggle, but she had the flash of fire in her eyes. She asked to talk to me. Here is what she said:

"Mr. Danforth, you have some influence, haven't you? Please, Mr. Danforth, urge the doctors to let me go back to my work. I'm strong enough. Those faces haunt me. They need my help. I can do a lot if I can only go back. . .""

Such pleading I never expect to hear again. I thought of my own daughter with her little children back home. I knew she would plead in the same way. The spirit can't be quenched, but what can a weak body do until strength and health are restored?

"No, Ruth," I said, "you can't go back to your work now. Your life has been miraculously spared for great days ahead. Obey the doctor's orders. Be a good soldier." She leaned back in her weak condition, crestfallen.

There's much to this story, but I've told enough. This girl used the energy she had in her, for she loved people, whether well, sick, rich, poor, in trouble, or out of it. She lived the abundant life of service. "She worked as if everything depended on her. She had faith as if everything depended on God."

How vividly such sharing adventures stand out in our memories. Riches or poverty are forgotten. Even Health and Mentality and Social Graces step aside before such devotion to an unselfish cause. I dare you to take your place among such of life's immortals as my Rich Little Rich Girl and my Rich Little Poor Girl. Make a masterpiece of your life.

And when you have dared to develop this ability to share with others you have discovered the meaning of an abundant life. Following the principle that our most valuable possessions are those which can be shared without lessening, those which, when shared, multiply; our least valuable possessions are those which, when divided, are diminished, then truly our physical, mental, social and spiritual selves multiply many times over when they are shared.

The more you practice this principle of daring and sharing, the more you find it in every contact of life. I heard my beloved pastor, Dr. Jay T. Stocking, who has now gone to his rich reward, preach a remarkable sermon on "The Investment of Life." He told the story of the loaves and fishes, but with a new interpretation. He stressed not the miracle of feeding the four thousand with a few loaves, but the attitude that takes account of resources possessed rather than difficulties presented. "Measure your powers, not your problems." What a dare in these adventurous days! When the disciples counted the crowd and petulantly complained that a few loaves were not enough to feed the multitudes, Jesus said, "How many loaves have ye? Don't look at the hillside - look at the basket. Don't count the crowd - count the loaves." He did not minimize the task. He suggested that if they could not feed four thousand people, they could at least the hunger of a few. They made a beginning and in using what they had under His direction, they acquired more than they had.

"We arrive here at a universal law of life and of God," said Dr. Stocking, "that resources and powers are given to those who use what resources and powers they have. Through the use of our muscles, our muscles grow and harden. Through the use of our mind, mental capacity increases; through the use of our spiritual powers these powers heighten.
We do not wear out the mind with thinking, or the soul with loving and showing mercy. It is within the experience of all of US that through using what we have we become possessed of larger abilities and resources. 'Don't count the multitude. Count the loaves.' "

Mahatma Gandhi never asks men for more than they can give, but he asks for all they can give.

I heard my friend, President Emeritus Wm, J. Hutchins of Berea College, give these thoughts to a graduating class.

"A few men build cities - the rest live in them.

"A few men project subways - the rest ride in them.

"A few men erect skyscrapers and factories - and the rest toil in them."

This book is written to you few who are going to accomplish things. You few who will dare to pioneer. You few who will dream of foundations and great super-structures to satisfy the needs of mankind. The rest will follow your leadership. You are the shepherds - the rest are the sheep. The shepherd loves his sheep. He faces danger. He knows hardship. There are stray lambs. He brings them back. Close your eyes and say to yourself, "I am one of the few. I have a leader's opportunity. I have a shepherd's responsibility. The rest are dependent upon me."

I'LL DARE TO SHARE WITH OTHERS

1. What talents have I which I could share with others?
2. In what way am I sharing my loaves with others?
3. How will I dare to use the life I have and share it with others?
4. Outline on a sheet of paper for myself a definite sharing program which I will start tomorrow.

LAUNCH OUT INTO THE DEEP

The four-square life that I've dared you to live isn't easy - it is hard. The masses, the 95%, will be content to go along their own way. Their plateau is comfortable. Why be disturbed or excited? But that other 4% and the Kingly 1% will never be held down until every unused capacity has been marshaled for service. What is it that lights the fuse of the 4% to the higher Leadership level and then that other 1% to the Kingly group? Why do the 95% never get their second wind? If the habits of the 95% keep them on their plateau, don't you think by grim determination, you, with your marvelous unused capacities, can form just as strong a habit to live on the 4% Leadership level or rise to the Kingly 1%? But it takes real stuff to do it.

When I sailed through the Caribbean Sea, I became steeped in the stories of old Panama. Why seek the Pacific beyond when there were treasures enough to spare on this side? But there was something more on the far shore . . . a new ocean to sail and the gold of the Incas! In between was that impenetrable Isthmus. There came Totten, the engineer, who spent five long years of untold difficulties and discouragement in building a railroad across that Isthmus. Through dense jungles infested by pestilential dangers, mosquitoes, flies, snakes, miasma everywhere in slimy ooze. "Every tie in the Panama Railroad represents the life of some man who paid the price of its construction with his life." Totten was stricken with yellow fever. For days he lingered between life and death. His Spanish doctor said there was no hope. Totten roused himself, and with that same indomitable courage that had marked his every step, said, "You are mistaken, sir; not yet. Yellow fever can't kill a Totten. I'm going to get well!" And he did. 4% and 1% stuff in him!

Then came the digging of the canal. DeLesseps, the famous Frenchman, had failed. The world said, "It can't be done." America purchased the Isthmus. President Theodore Roosevelt appointed George W. Goethals to build the canal. He had the reputation of never quitting. The world flippantly said: "Let George do it." Colonel Goethals "put to the full test the fearless courage that was the measure of the man." The canal was completed. "George did it." No 95% plateau levels for this George.

But George didn't do it without the help of another fearless man. William C. Gorgas, an American Army doctor, was selected to fight malaria and yellow fever. He scanned the record of twenty thousand who had died from these pestilential diseases. One report showed that five hundred young engineers came from France to Panama and "not one lived to draw his first month's pay." Then began Dr. Gorgas' most amazing campaign. He was ridiculed, called a mosquito chaser; but Gorgas "concentrated his sleepless energies upon one single aim - the destruction of the infecting mosquitoes, and he won what was unquestionably the greatest triumph in preventive medicine. A campaign waged for less than six months wiped out a scourge that had afflicted this region for at least four hundred years." Had he allowed ridicule and opposition to overcome his courage, the Panama Canal might not have been built.

Courage for your tasks. That's what's needed. Courage of the lasting kind, too. Many start. Few finish. Many "mount up with wings like eagles" but only the select few continue to "walk without fainting."

You adventurous spirits will meet obstacles, but dare to map out a program of life with a sense of direction, but with no sense of obstacles.

Alexander the Great heard of India's fabulous wealth and splendor. There he would go. He had no maps but he had an objective and a sense of direction. Rivers and mountains and warlike nations had no terrors for him. Through the Khyber Pass he went with no sense of obstacles. His eyes were on his destination.

Caesar saw Britain - not the gruelling marches, treacherous tribes, and danger on every hand between him and his goal. He had an objective and a sense of direction. Napoleon saw Italy but not the Alps. Washington saw the Hessians at Trenton. A smaller man would have seen the ice-filled Delaware.

The 95% see the obstacles. The 4% and the 1% see the objective. Small men painstakingly survey the first obstacle which dwarfs their natures and foreshortens their vision. Great men with a sense of direction have that confidence and determination which trample obstacles under foot.

History records the successes of men with objectives and a sense of direction. Oblivion is the position of small men overwhelmed by obstacles.

Living the Four-Square life through your Dares gives you a sense of direction and sweeps obstacles out of your path. Your adventurous life has just begun. It takes more than saying you are going to do it to achieve. Theodore Roosevelt said, "There must be more shooting and less shouting; fewer words and more real work. Words will not plow a field; words will not build a home; words will not develop a great humanity, nor build a great nation." There is discipline ahead. Walking with the army and wearing a uniform doesn't make a man a soldier.

Dare to make a start. All the plans in the world will not help you so much as one small deed. This book will not have served its purpose unless it starts you living the complete life. It is human to put things off. It is divine to start things off. Your daring program begins not next month, not next week, not even tomorrow. I dare you to begin to live the Four-Square life today.

There's Hero Stuff in you. I dare you to get it out. Use your imagination as you read this football dope.

" . . . and the coach kicks every man out on the field and tells him to go to it. He keeps right on working them back and forth until their tongues hang out and they think they can't make another down. Then he works them some more, and some more, and finally ends up in a sprint around the track.

The result is that every man brings out everything that is in him. The fast and fearless step into their strides and replace the halfbacks that aren't any good. Finally there is a great team and a great game and a great score. And the man who made those two touchdowns on that muddy day in November becomes a Hero and stays one all the rest of his life and every man on the team is proud."

"Pass the ball to me," do I hear you say? Pass it to you with those weights on your shoulders and shackles on your feet which prevent you from moving? No sir! The man with the ball must be in fighting trim. Go back to those inflexible rules of the four-square life in the preceding chapters. Master them. Get on the Varsity Team of life. Face your tasks. Launch out. Take the risk. Dare to do.

I would encourage many little Dares. You will need them to bolster up that one great, big, all-absorbing Dare of your life. Let me look you squarely in the eyes, hear your Dare, and learn of the purpose behind it, and I'll gamble I can take your measure. If I see the light of battle in your eyes and catch something of a dominant inner urge, then I know you are on your way.

Many are good starters but poor finishers. The streets are full of people who started out but fell by the wayside. "This man began to build, but was not able to finish." Launching your ship is a gala occasion, but the storms and waves are the tests. "I'm afraid you won't be able to make it," whispers a little Imp who constantly tries to poison your mind. Knock such fears galley-west. Those who dare - take risks, but so do those who do not dare. Not the risks of shipwreck and failure, but the risks of rust and decay. Do you remember the story of the Covered Wagon crossing the plains toward the Golden West?

"The Coward never started;
The Weak died on the way;
Only the Strong came through!"

There will be times when you will want to quit, when you will consign me and my dares to a warmer climate. But you can't quit. You have unused capacities that cry out within you. You are made of 4% Leadership stuff - yes, maybe you belong to the Kingly 1%. John Paul Jones, when ordered to surrender, said, "We've just begun to fight!" Did Admiral Farragut weaken with hidden mines in his path? "Damn the torpedoes. Full steam ahead!" was his command. Determination to win decides the issue. During the war in France, one of our officers, after being asked the question, "Can we hold them?" answered, "Can we hold them? We will go through them and smash them."

May I say again that the real cause of strength under baffling conditions comes right back to your four-square life. That's the secret I must tell. Those four hard chapters contain the very heart of life. I have seen the test come in business and in war. In my Division in France we had some Tennessee mountain boys. When Hell was turned loose they were bewildered. They knew two things, however; they knew their rifles and they knew how to shoot straight. When fundamentals begin to grip you, when you have made the four-square life your life, all Hell may break, but you will dare to reach your goal.

Let me finish this chapter by again impressing on you from a business point of view what I've tried to say in the preceding pages.

Capitalize four-square living just as bankers or manufacturers capitalize their assets. Use your physical strength. Put it behind your dare. Keep enough in reserve for emergencies. You can go far using your teeming physical energy. Corral your brain power. When you have learned to face facts and think straight, you can mix brains with that fine body of yours and have two arrows to shoot. Making friends and holding them by a winsome personality along with an alert mind and strong body, you have three powers at your command. You who dare, don't waste. The four-fold life is yours because underneath a body which is under control and a mind keen as a brier and a personality that sparkles at every contact, there is a religion with truth, honesty and purity as its base.

Will you, who dare, use one, or two . . . or all?

Make up your mind to Dare. These ideas aren't worth a thing to you unless carried out. The 20th Century Limited would stand forever in the station if they didn't give it steam. Unless you dare, you are on a dead center. How would you expect your ship to come in if you never sent one out? It was ridiculous for David to fight Goliath. Foolishness for Columbus to try to sail around the earth. Nonsense for the Wright Brothers to dream they could fly. But suppose they hadn't tried?

Master the five previous chapters. Who will be content today without striving for all that the four-square life has to offer - physical strength, mental alertness, a magnetic personality, and a religion that fits us for the highest service?

Achieve Greatly through a clear and powerful urge to accomplish something notable - through a superior persistence; through marked faith in yourself: "I can do great things if I try"; high capacity for self-improvement; energy great enough to sustain in long, tremendous drives; high enthusiasm; intellectual curiosity - the itch to understand; marked dexterity of eye, hand, tongue, and body; creative imagination. These are some of Professor Pitkin's thoughts which, coupled with his definition of Achievement, will open up vast possibilities. "Achievement is distinguished successful endeavor, usually in the face of difficulties. As such it always possesses two characteristics; first, a certain superiority of aim, and, secondly, exceptional skill in execution."

Never give up until you have released your unused capacities for service and shared your gifts with others. One enkindled spirit can set hundreds on fire.

I want to lift you to your peak performance whatever that is. I want you to do some long-range thinking, to have an imagination to see far beyond anything I have said. If only one in a thousand gets the big idea of a Dare, then I should be happy. I know I would if that one were my own boy. We haven't scratched the surface of human reservoirs yet. Do you wonder that I'm urging you to Dare? Picture anyone looking at the rushing, tumbling waters of Niagara Falls - power beyond imagination even - and saying, "I'll take a cupful." Or that echo of a little midget purring, "Just a thimbleful for me." Oftentimes I find myself offering up a prayer, "Lord, open the eyes of the blind, quicken the imagination of the weak."

I read a part of the manuscript of "I Dare You" to a young friend. "How very interesting," he said. Gosh! If I've spent my time writing this to no greater purpose than interesting somebody, then I've failed miserably. Unless this book stirs you to Action and makes you want to get somewhere, then the daring adventure of magnificent four-square living has been presented by a mighty poor salesman.

ENVOI

**Just a final word to you who have read
"I Dare You": If you don't DARE,
then it must be pretty much my fault.
But you MUST DARE. You must do
something. You can't put this book
down without determining in a personal
way to start something. Others have
grown by DARING. So must you. It's
time for ACTION for you. Come on.
What's your DARE?**

I DARE AND SHARE

It is my hope that every reader has gotten something out of the preceding chapters. Even if some haven't, I'm not going to give up. For a number of years in my business, we have been setting goals. Some didn't relish the idea at first. Bill didn't like to take a personal inventory. Mary didn't want to set a goal and then be urged to reach it. But many of those very ones who disliked the idea most have received the most benefit. The fact is that those who have set goals have advanced far more than the lukewarm or the belligerent. I have observed that setting a goal makes no appeal to the mediocre. But to those fired with an ambition really to achieve greatly, setting a goal becomes a program that stirs the inner soul to action.

If you have that urge to go a step farther, I want you to go back to pages 35, 62, 79 and 91 and check over your Physical, Mental, Social and Religious Dares. In daring to "Beat Your Best," you are going to need all sides of your checker.

With grim determination plan the most healthful, most thrilling, most romantic and most spiritual year of your life.

Let me sound a warning. A Dare based on half facts and only half thought through is less than half a Dare. Build your Dare in your own way, but do it seriously face to face with yourself, alone. Don't be tempted to Dare beyond your capacity. That may entail disappointment and discouragement. On the other hand, make your Dare worthy of your best. The ambitious son of a carthorse never wins in the Derby races. Only thoroughbreds dominate there.

There is another admonition I would like to give to you eager crusaders now starting out on a daring program. There are two great parts to any program - the start and the finish. You have made your start and I want to urge you to finish. Industry, the professions, the world, are crying for men who can finish things. A friend told me the following incident:

"Last fall I saw a horse race at the Nebraska State Fair. A white-faced horse got the pole and took the lead. At the quarter he struck mud and the second horse passed him. I wish you could have seen that white-faced horse run the last half- mile. The finish was close, but he won."

You are going to start this race on a high crest of enthusiasm. You are going to strike mud. Some are going to pass you, but during that last half-mile run as you never ran before. It's down that last stretch that you white-faced horses must run home with everything that's in you.

In order to make your Dares definite, write them down. Fix a date for their accomplishment. With that courageous spirit which banishes all fear, you must reach your goal.

Finally, if this Dare program has helped you, why not pass it along to others?

I don't want you just to distribute a book. I want you to stimulate a life. If the Dare idea is worth anything it will grow through your influence and mine.

"I Dare You" has been distributed by business executives to their employees, by colleges, schools, Y. M. C. A.s, Scouts and from friend to friend. It has been circulated by those who have taken a Dare. Thus far the "I Dare You" Committee has handled the distribution.

This book is my contribution to the development of the youth of our land. I do not want any royalties or profit from it. Whatever amounts are received for it through the "I Dare You" Committee after all expenses are paid will go to the American Youth Foundation.

If you count yourself among those who have Dared, then you will begin to share the "I Dare You" life with others.

Now that you have read this book, what are you going to do about it?

You with an Ambition on Fire-

You with a Brilliant Career before you-

You with Creative Ability as yet untapped-

You with an Executive Mind destined to carry you far-

You who have already Dared but haven't as yet learned to Share-

What are YOU going to do right now to lift yourself out of the crowd and make something significant out of your life?

In the pages that follow, men who have achieved tell how the "I Dare You" spirit has gripped them.

Will you Dare yourself?

Will you pass the Dare spirit along to others?

What you do today and in the immediate days that follow is the thing that will prove whether or not you possess the spirit of the priceless few who DARE.

Wm. H. Danforth.

SIR WILFRED T. GRENFELL, K.C.M.G.

Sir Wilfred Grenfell who dared to face the cold of bleak Labrador to share his rich life with others read "I Dare You." Note his comments:

Mr. Danforth's manuscript comes from his soul and from experience. I will gladly endorse himself, his ideas, his business methods, and his courageous attempts to put his creeds into writing, as well as practice.

Just leaving for Labrador. The reading of this manuscript has done me good. Please convey my affectionate greetings to Mr. Danforth. He is one of the men whom you feel better for meeting and I hope to renew acquaintance.

Later Sir Wilfred wrote:

It has been my privilege to visit the Purina factory and see the business, and study the philosophy which Mr. Danforth's life has created. I have talked to his workers and have been thrilled by their enthusiasm. Far beyond its excellent food products, it is a factory of human character.

Now I have read Mr. Danforth's DARE book, and I have met Mr. Danforth personally, and both experiences have left me a better man. Of this I am certain - that in whatever rank or business or activity a man is engaged, he will be a better man for reading this book, and ten times a better one if he acts upon it.

"I Dare You" is more than a book. It is an awakening thought that stirs you to do more than you have ever done before. Sir Wilfred spread this doctrine. You are spreading it, too.

SHERWOOD EDDY

Sherwood Eddy faced ten thousand angry Communists in Moscow. He picked up the challenge of a whole nation's religious disbelief. He belongs to the Dare group. He writes:

As a senior at Yale, a man said to me, "You have one life to live. What are you going to do with it?" That question completely changed my future. That is the question my friend, William H. Danforth, has been asking people ever since I have known him. That is the question he asks you in this book, "I Dare You." But better still, he answers it by giving you a plan that will help you invest your one life to better advantage. You, Youth with your wealth of health, intelligence, ambition, friends, possibilities - you have everything, everything save one, and that is experience. Here experience speaks to you from the pages of his own life.

Mr. Danforth gets more out of life than a dozen average men. I know of no busier businessman. Yet he has found time to travel with me into many interesting corners of the world. Abundant health, keen appreciation of the spiritual, an eager interest in life as a whole and an intense passion of worthwhile accomplishment in all spheres in life are qualities that particularly make it worth our while to consider well his daring plan of life.

Now that you have read "I Dare You," like Sherwood Eddy, you will be passing along Dares to others because you have taken big Dares yourself.

MAJOR J. W. WOOLDRIDGE

Major Wooldridge was a Comrade in Arms in France with Mr. Danforth in World War I. Many times wounded and many times decorated - the Distinguished Service Cross, Distinguished Service Medal, Legion of Honor of France, Croix de Guerre with Palm and Italian War Cross, Major Wooldridge knows the meaning of "Dare". He writes:

Don't Read This Book! If you are one who has made up his mind that he doesn't need to improve himself - don't read this book!

If you have no need for an objective in life, a goal that will become a "Magnificent Obsession," one that awakens you in the morning with a desire to do things - don't read this book!

If you are satisfied with your body and do not want to strengthen your mind, build up your character and spiritual resistance - don't read this book!

If you don't want to develop your charm and personality, add more friends to your list and be a better friend - don't read this book!

If you have no desire to bring out the latent powers that are in you and understand why the fountain of spiritual sharing increases with use - don't read this book!

If you want to think it's none of your business to help others to build pride, courage and devotion to higher ideals - don't read this book!

Generally speaking, I mean, if you are entirely satisfied with what you are now -don't read this book!

But, if you are one who would know you have in you those qualities which can put you in the 5 per cent class; if you want to awaken the slumbering resources of your mind; if you would know that the true measure of individual worth is in performance, not merely possessions; if you would make the world better for having lived in it; if you would meet a great man, who has had great dreams and moulded them into great achievements on whatever field of life he has played the game (I mean, if you would meet Mr. Danforth, man to man and face to face, as I have met him on the field of battle); if you would meet and know a man who will inspire you to make yourself bigger than the things that can happen to you - Read This Book!

Those of us in the old Third Division will bear testimony that Mr. Danforth was always in the thick of things. Shot and shell and mud were no terrors for him. I know his daring theory worked here. He dared and shared and made every day an adventure.

Read this book once to yourself and once aloud - and I dare you, from then on, to make it a text of life itself. You will!

Today you are joining the "I Dare You" ranks. Today with Major Wooldridge you fight the glorious battle of "Dare and Share."

JOHN L. ALEXANDER

If you are interested in the Boy Scouts, you will catch the ringing message of John L. Alexander, who was the first National Secretary of the Boy Scouts of America. Dr. Alexander until his death was Director of the American Youth Foundation and knows the heart of Daring Youth. He says:

This book breathes the spirit of achievement in action. This inspiring philosophy of Mr. Danforth says that a man's best is nothing less than his growing capacity. Personally, I have seen this compelling idea at work in the lives of youth in the office, in camp and in school. It has given a new meaning of life to hundreds. "I Dare You" will vitally challenge the thousands outside the reach of his voice. Mr. Danforth is a master in kindling this inner urge for creative effort in the lives of youth. The spirit of its pages is the written inspiration of his personal contacts with individual youth.

DR. PAUL DEKRUIF

Dr. Paul deKruif who through his books, "Microbe Hunters" and "Hunger Fighters" challenges our creative ability, shares the "Daring" of his friend, Mr. Danforth. Dr. deKruif writes:

The manuscript of Mr. Danforth's "I Dare You" has given me much pleasure, deals with a fundamental that is too often ignored in school and college instruction, written in a style that can be read and assimilated by a sixteen-year-old boy, fixing values in his life which should be learned from a practical teacher of Mr. Danforth's experience rather than in a college.

To keep in step with so daring a thinker as Paul deKruif challenges our best. Every page of his books reflects a "Daring Spirit."

JAMES SAXON CHILDERS

Mr. Danforth often talks of "Jimmy", a Southern boy who came to one of the summer camps. "Jimmy" had the Dare germ in him. Mr. Danforth saw it, dared him to go to college. "Jimmy" graduated, won a Rhodes Scholarship, distinguished himself at Oxford, travelled around the world as a news correspondent. Today he is an author of many stimulating books. Here's what James Saxon Childers says:

I first saw William H. Danforth late one afternoon at a camp in Wisconsin. "Tell me, son," he said, "'where are you going to college?" I told him I couldn't go. "Go on to college," he said. "I dare you."

Four years later Mr. Danforth visited Oberlin College. "What are you going to do after you're graduated, Jimmy?" he asked. I told him I was going to work. "Don't do that. Study some more. Go to a university. Go to Oxford." I told him I couldn't possibly go to a university, least of all could I go to Oxford. "I dare you, Jimmy," Mr. Danforth said.

Four years later he took tea with me in my rooms at Oxford. "And now what, Jimmy?" he asked. I told him I was going to get a job of some kind, though I admitted I wanted to write. "Then write," Mr. Danforth said. "But I can't write," I said. "The thought of writing terrifies me." He looked at me in that way of his - it rather makes you want to get out of your chair and go do something, anything, but most of all something of which you're afraid. "Write me a book," he said. "I dare you to write me a book and publish it within two years. I dare you."

And he's not satisfied. He's still throwing his dares, still driving as he has always driven himself. My greatest wish - and this is written in utmost sincerity - is that I might dare the big jobs as he has dared, and that I might carry them through in the same fine way he has carried through to the success so justly his.

CAROLYN D. SMILEY

Long ago a great challenge came to Carolyn D. Smiley. She heard the missionary call from far off India. She dared to go half way around the world to a strange people, to a new language, to a life of Daring. She writes:

Some of us love to be dared. All of us love a fine, daring personality. This book is full of striking experiences of human beings who dared to think and do big things in the world. It is written in a quick, colorful, vivid style, so in keeping with the 'I Dare you' spirit of the author.

As she carried the gospel to action so do we pass along the challenge to a Daring Life.

WALTER WILLIAMS

A successful editor, a great statesman and a noted educator, Walter Williams, former President of the University of Missouri, caught the note of a "happy warrior" in "I Dare You":

I am pleased to have been given the opportunity to examine the manuscript by Mr. William H. Danforth. It is a vital message thus put forth and will, I am confident, be of large effectiveness for good. It challenges the soul of every reader -this expression of the philosophy of a happy warrior for religion.

Is there a more fertile field to sow seeds of Daring than in the "Dare" colleges of our land? Fortunate are we if as teachers we can put the "Dare" spark into the formative lives of youth.

REV. JAY T. STOCKING, D.D.

What a debt we owe our ministers! Mr. Danforth had a close relationship with his beloved late pastor, Dr. Jay T. Dr. Stocking practiced what he preached. He gave Dares and he took Dares:

I have read with much interest and pleasure the galley proof of Mr. Danforth's new book, "I Dare You." Like all of Mr. Danforth's writings, it is stimulating and energizing. It is the wholesome gospel of self-development through self-investment.

This is a book that one should not read just before going to bed. I read it at such a time and I had to take a hot bath to relax myself. It should be read in the morning when the day is before one and one can do something about it. It is too exciting a book for a nightcap.

The book should not be read by people who want to think that they have arrived, or that they are doing pretty well, or who desire to settle clown. It is a very unsettling book. The satisfied will find in it no satisfaction.

No one has a right to say "I Dare You" except one who will take the dare himself. Mr. Danforth is such a man - eager, unsatisfied, aspiring and young. He is only asking others to join him in his everlasting quest for the better and bigger man who is in every one of us.

Many ministers are preaching "I Dare You" sermons once a year on Youth Sundays. "I Dare You" has also been taken as a theme for many Young People's two-day conferences.

CARL R. GRAY

The great Union Pacific Railroad had as its chief executive, Chairman Carl R. Gray. He knew men. Catch his daring:

Nothing great has ever been accomplished unless somebody first dared to do it. Our early railroad pioneers had visions of two ribbons of steel stretched toward the setting sun and dared to make their dreams come true. Without daring men, our country would still be a wilderness. I have seen what Mr. Danforth has done in daring those in his own organization to superior achievements. I dare you to let this idea take hold of you. You can never rest on the same plateau again.

Heavy responsibility lies on the shoulders of such an executive. Others depend on him for inspiration. To follow in the footsteps of a leader like Carl R. Gray, requires that our business executives be charged with the "I Dare You" spirit.

To Our DARING FRIENDS

I DARE YOU has been privately printed for youth over the land. Since there was a growing public demand for I DARE YOU, Wm. H. Danforth gave it to the "I Dare You" Committee, and any profits from its sales go to the American Youth Foundation.

I DARE YOU has proved especially valuable to give to young people for birthday or graduation presents. Business executives have found it highly effective in stimulating their salesmen to increased efficiency. Any age group will profit by reading it.

As A Man Thinketh

by James Allen

TABLE OF CONTENTS

FOREWORD

This little volume (the result of meditation and experience) is not intended as an exhaustive treatise on the much written upon subject of the power of thought. It is suggestive rather than explanatory, its object being to stimulate men and women to the discovery and perception of the truth that - "They themselves are makers of themselves" - by virtue of the thoughts which they choose and encourage. That mind is the master weaver, both of the inner garment of character and the outer garment of circumstance, and that, as they may have hitherto woven in ignorance and pain, they may now weave in enlightenment and happiness.

JAMES ALLEN

THOUGHT AND CHARACTER

The aphorism, "As a man thinketh in his heart so is he," not only embraces the whole of a man's being, but is so comprehensive as to reach out to every condition and circumstance of his life. A man is literally what he thinks, his character being the complete sum of all his thoughts.

As the plant springs from, and could not be without the seed, so every act of a man springs from the hidden seeds of thought, and could not have appeared without them. This applies equally to those acts called "spontaneous" and "unpremeditated" as to those which are deliberately executed.

Act is the blossom of thought, and joy and suffering are its fruits; thus does a man garner in the sweet and bitter fruitage of his own husbandry.

Thought in the mind hath made us. What we are by thought what we wrought and built. If a man's mind hath evil thoughts, pain comes on him as comes the wheel the ox behind ... If one endures in purity of thought, joy follows him as his own shadow, sure.

Man is a growth by law, and not a creation by artifice, and cause and effect is as absolute and undeviating in the hidden realm of thought as in the world of visible and material things. A noble and Godlike character is not a thing of favor or chance, but is the natural result of continued effort in right thinking, the effect of long-cherished association with Godlike thoughts. An ignoble and bestial character, by the same process, is the result of the continued harboring of groveling thoughts.

Man is made or unmade by himself; in the armory of thought he forges the weapons by which he destroys himself. He also fashions the tools with which he builds for himself heavenly mansions of joy and strength and peace. By the right choice and true application of thought, man ascends to the Divine Perfection; by the abuse and wrong application of thought, he descends below the level of the beast. Between these two extremes are all the grades of character, and man is their maker and master.

Of all the beautiful truths pertaining to the soul which have been restored and brought to light in this age, none is more gladdening or fruitful of divine promise and confidence than this - that man is the master of thought, the molder of character, and maker and shaper of condition, environment, and destiny.

As a being of Power, Intelligence, and Love, and the lord of his own thoughts, man holds the key to every situation, and contains within himself that transforming and regenerative agency by which he may make himself what he wills. Man is always the master, even in his weakest and most abandoned state; but in his weakness and degradation he is the foolish master who misgoverns his "household."   When he begins to reflect upon his condition, and to search diligently for the Law upon which his being is established, he then becomes the wise master, directing his energies with intelligence, and fashioning his thoughts to fruitful issues. Such is the conscious master, and man can only thus become by discovering within himself the laws of thought - - which discovery is totally a matter of application, self-analysis, and experience.

Only by much searching and mining are gold and diamonds obtained, and man can find every truth connected with his being if he will dig deep into the mine of his soul. And that he is the maker of his character, the molder of his life, and the builder of his destiny, he may unerringly prove: if he will watch, control, and alter his thoughts, tracing their effects upon himself, upon others, and upon his life and circumstances; if he will link cause and effect by patient practice and investigation, utilizing his every experience, even to the most trivial, as a means of obtaining that knowledge of himself. In this direction, as in no other, is the law absolute that "He that seeketh findeth; and to him that knocketh it shall be opened". For only by patience, practice, and ceaseless importunity can a man enter the Door of the Temple of Knowledge.

EFFECT OF THOUGHT ON CIRCUMSTANCES

A man's mind may be likened to a garden, which may be intelligently cultivated or allowed to run wild; but whether cultivated or neglected, it must, and will, bring forth. If no useful seeds are put into it, then an abundance of useless weed seeds will fall therein, and will continue to produce their kind.

Just as a gardener cultivates his plot, keeping it free from weeds, and growing the flowers and fruits which he requires, so may a man tend the garden of his mind, weeding out all the wrong, useless, and impure thoughts, and cultivating toward perfection the flowers and fruits of right, useful, and pure thoughts. By pursuing this process, a man sooner or later discovers that he is the master gardener of his soul, the director of his life. He also reveals, within himself, the laws of thought, and understands with ever-increasing accuracy, how the thought forces and mind elements operate in the shaping of his character, circumstances, and destiny.

Thought and character are one, and as character can only manifest and discover itself through environment and circumstance, the outer conditions of a person's life will always be found to be harmoniously related to his inner state. This does not mean that a man's circumstances at any given time are an indication of his entire character, but that those circumstances are so intimately connected with some vital thought element within himself that, for the time being, they are indispensable to his development.

Every man is where he is by the law of his being. The thoughts which he has built into his character have brought him there, and in the arrangement of his life there is no element of chance, but all is the result of a law which can not err. This is just as true of those who feel "out of harmony" with their surroundings as of those who are contented with them.

As the progressive and evolving being, man is where he is that he may learn that he may grow; and as he learns the spiritual lesson which any circumstance contains for him, it passes away and gives place to other circumstances.

Man is buffeted by circumstances so long as he believes himself to be the creature of outside conditions. But when he realizes that he may command the hidden soil and seeds of his being out of which circumstances grow, he then becomes the rightful master of himself.

That circumstances grow out of thought every man knows who has for any length of time practiced self-control and self-purification, for he will have noticed that the alteration in his circumstances has been in exact ratio with his altered mental condition. So true is this that when a man earnestly applies himself to remedy the defects in his character, and makes swift and marked progress, he passes rapidly through a succession of vicissitudes.

The soul attracts that which it secretly harbors; that which it loves, and also that which it fears. It reaches the height of its cherished aspirations. It falls to the level of its unchastened desires - and circumstances are the means by which the soul receives its own.

Every thought seed sown or allowed to fall into the mind and to take root there, produces its own blossoming sooner or later into act, and bearing its own fruitage of opportunity and circumstance. Good thoughts bear good fruit, bad thoughts bad fruit.

The outer world of circumstance shapes itself to the inner world of thought, and both pleasant and unpleasant external conditions are factors which make for the ultimate good of the individual. As the reaper of his own harvest, man learns both by suffering and bliss.

A man does not come to the almshouse or the jail by the tyranny of fate of circumstance, but by the pathway of groveling thoughts and base desires. Nor does a pure-minded man fall suddenly into crime by stress of any mere external force; the criminal thought had long been secretly fostered in the heart, and the hour of opportunity revealed its gathered power.

Circumstance does not make the man; it reveals him to himself. No such conditions can exist as descending into vice and its attendant sufferings apart from vicious inclinations, or ascending into virtue and its pure happiness without the continued cultivation of virtuous aspirations. And man, therefore, as the Lord and master of thought, is the maker of himself, the shaper and author of environment. Even at birth the soul comes to its own, and through every step of its earthly pilgrimage, it attracts those combinations of conditions which reveal itself, which are the reflections of its own purity and impurity, its strength and weakness.

Men do not attract that which they want, but that which they are. Their whims, fancies, and ambitions are thwarted at every step, but their inmost thoughts and desires are fed with their own food, be it foul or clean. The "divinity that shapes our ends" is in ourselves - it is our very self. Man is manacled only by himself. Thought and action are the jailers of Fate - they imprison, being base. They are also the angels of Freedom - they liberate, being noble. Not what he wishes and prays for does a man get, but what he justly earns. His wishes and prayers are only gratified and answered when they harmonize with his thoughts and actions.

In the light of this truth, what, then, is the meaning of "fighting against circumstances"? It means that a man is continually revolting against an effect without, while all the time he is nourishing and preserving its cause in his heart. That cause may take the form of a conscious vice or an unconscious weakness; but whatever it is, it stubbornly retards the efforts of its possessor, and thus calls aloud for remedy.

Men are anxious to improve their circumstances, but are unwilling to improve themselves. They therefore remain bound. The man who does not shrink from self-crucifixion can never fail to accomplish the object upon which his heart is set. This is as true of earthly as of heavenly things. Even the man whose sole object is to acquire wealth must be prepared to make great personal sacrifices before he can accomplish his object; and how much more so he who would realize a strong and well-poised life?

Here is a man who is wretchedly poor. He is extremely anxious that his surroundings and home comforts should be improved. Yet all the time he shirks his work, and considers he is justified in trying to deceive his employer on the ground of the insufficiency of his wages. Such a man does not understand the simplest rudiments of those principles which are the basis of true prosperity. He is not only totally unfitted to rise out of his wretchedness, but is actually attracting to himself a still deeper wretchedness by dwelling in, and acting out, indolent, deceptive, and unmanly thoughts.

Here is a rich man who is the victim of a painful and persistent disease as the result of gluttony. He is willing to give large sums of money to get rid of it, but he will not sacrifice his gluttonous desires. He wants to gratify his taste for rich and unnatural foods and have his health as well. Such a man is totally unfit to have health, because he has not yet learned the first principles of a healthy life.

Here is an employer of labor who adopts crooked measures to avoid paying the regulation wage, and, in the hope of making larger profits, reduces the wages of his work people. Such a man is altogether unfitted for prosperity. And when he finds himself bankrupt, both as regards reputation and riches, he blames circumstances, not knowing that he is the sole author of his condition.

I have introduced these three cases merely as illustrative of the truth that man is the cause (though nearly always unconsciously) of his circumstances. That, while aiming at the good end, he is continually frustrating its accomplishment by encouraging thoughts and desires which cannot possibly harmonize with that end. Such cases could be multiplied and varied almost indefinitely, but this is not necessary. The reader can, if he so resolves, trace the action of the laws of thought in his own mind and life, and until this is done, mere external facts cannot serve as a ground of reasoning.

Circumstances, however, are so complicated, thought is so deeply rooted, and the conditions of happiness vary so vastly with individuals, that a man's entire soul condition (although it may be known to himself) cannot be judged by another from the external aspect of his life alone.

A man may be honest in certain directions, yet suffer privations. A man may be dishonest in certain directions, yet acquire wealth. But the conclusion usually formed that the one man fails because of his particular honesty, and that the other prospers because of his particular dishonesty, is the result of a superficial judgment, which assumes that the dishonest man is almost totally corrupt, and honest man almost entirely virtuous. In the light of a deeper knowledge and wider experience, such judgment is found to be erroneous. The dishonest man may have some admirable virtues which the other does not possess; and the honest man obnoxious vices which are absent in the other. The honest man reaps the good results of his honest thoughts and acts; he also brings upon himself the sufferings which his vices produce. The dishonest man likewise garners his own suffering and happiness.

It is pleasing to human vanity to believe that one suffers because of one's virtue. But not until a man has extirpated every sickly, bitter, and impure thought from his mind, and washed every sinful stain from his soul, can he be in a position to know and declare that his sufferings are the result of his good, and not of his bad qualities. And on the way to that supreme perfection, he will have found working in his mind and life, the Great Law which is absolutely just, and which cannot give good for evil, evil for good. Possessed of such knowledge, he will then know, looking back upon his past ignorance and blindness, that his life is, and always was, justly ordered, and that all his past experiences, good and bad, were the equitable outworking of his evolving, yet unevolved self.

Good thoughts and actions can never produce bad results. Bad thoughts and actions can never produce good results. This is but saying that nothing can come from corn but corn, nothing from nettles but nettles. Men understand this law in the natural world, and work with it. But few understand it in the mental and moral world (though its operation there is just as simple and undeviating), and they, therefore, do not cooperate with it.

Suffering is always the effect of wrong thought in some direction. It is an indication that the individual is out of harmony with himself, with the Law of his being. The sole and supreme use of suffering is to purify, to burn out all that is useless and impure. Suffering ceases for him who is pure. There could be not object in burning gold after the dross had been removed, and perfectly pure and enlightened being could not suffer.

The circumstances which a man encounters with suffering are the result of his own mental inharmony. The circumstances which a man encounters with blessedness, not material possessions, is the measure of right thought. Wretchedness, not lack of material possessions, is the measure of wrong thought. A man may be cursed and rich; he may be blessed and poor. Blessedness and riches are only joined together when the riches are rightly and wisely used. And the poor man only descends into wretchedness when he regards his lot as a burden unjustly imposed.

Indigence and indulgence are the two extremes of wretchedness. They are both equally unnatural and the result of mental disorder. A man is not rightly conditioned until he is a happy, healthy, and prosperous being. And happiness, health, and prosperity are the result of a harmonious adjustment of the inner with the outer, of the man with his surroundings.

A man only begins to be a man when he ceases to whine and revile, and commences to search for the hidden justice which regulates his life. And as he adapts his mind to that regulating factor, he ceases to accuse others as the cause of his condition, and builds himself up in strong and noble thoughts. He ceases to kick against circumstances, but begins to use them as aids, to his more rapid progress, and as a means of discovering the hidden powers and possibilities within himself.

Law, not confusion, is the dominating principle in the universe. Justice, not injustice, is the soul and substance of life. And righteousness, not corruption, is the molding and moving force in the spiritual government of the world. This being so, man has but to right himself to find that the universe is right; and during the process of putting himself right, he will find that as he alters his thoughts toward things and other people, things and other people will alter toward him.

The proof of this truth is in every person, and it therefore admits of easy investigation by systematic introspection and self-analysis. Let a man radically alter his thoughts, and he will be astonished at the rapid transformation it will effect in the material conditions of his life.

Men imagine that thought can be kept secret, but it cannot. It rapidly crystallizes into habit, and habit solidifies into habits of drunkenness and sensuality, which solidify into circumstances of destitution and disease. Impure thoughts of every kind crystallize into enervating and confusing habits, which solidify into distracting and adverse circumstances. Thoughts of fear, doubt, and indecision crystallize into weak, unmanly, and irresolute habits, which solidify into circumstances of failure, indigence, and slavish dependence.

Lazy thoughts crystallize into habits of uncleanliness and dishonesty, which solidify into circumstances of foulness and beggary. Hateful and condemnatory thoughts crystallize into habits of accusation and violence, which solidify into circumstances of injury and persecution. Selfish thoughts of all kinds crystallize into habits of self-seeking, which solidify into circumstances more of less distressing.

On the other hand, beautiful thoughts of all crystallize into habits of grace and kindliness, which solidify into genial and sunny circumstances. Pure thoughts crystallize into habits of temperance and self-control, which solidify into circumstances of repose and peace. Thoughts of courage, self-reliance, and decision crystallize into manly habits, which solidify into circumstances of success, plenty, and freedom.

Energetic thoughts crystallize into habits of cleanliness and industry, which solidify into circumstances of pleasantness. Gentle and forgiving thoughts crystallize into habits of gentleness, which solidify into protective and preservative circumstances. Loving and unselfish thoughts crystallize into habits of self-forgetfulness for others, which solidify into circumstances of sure and abiding prosperity and true riches.

A particular train of thought persisted in, be it good or bad, cannot fail to produce its results on the character and circumstances. A man cannot directly choose his circumstances, but he can choose his thoughts, and so indirectly, yet surely, shape his circumstances.

Nature helps every man to the gratification of the thoughts which he most encourages, and opportunities are presented which will most speedily bring to the surface both the good and evil thoughts.

Let a man cease from his sinful thoughts, and all the world will soften toward him, and be ready to help him. Let him put away his weakly and sickly thoughts, and lo! Opportunities will spring up on every hand to aid his strong resolves. Let him encourage good thoughts, and no hard fate shall bind him down to wretchedness and shame. The world is your kaleidoscope, and the varying combinations of colors which at every succeeding moment it presents to you are the exquisitely adjusted pictures of your evermoving thoughts.

You will be what you will to be; Let failure find its false content in that poor word, "environment," but spirit scorns it, and is free.
It masters time, it conquers space;
It cows that boastful trickster, Chance, and bids the tyrant circumstance uncrown, and fill a servant's place.
The human Will, that force unseen,
The offspring of a deathless Soul,
Can hew a way to any goal,
Though walls of granite intervene.

Be not impatient in delay, but wait as one who understands.

EFFECT OF THOUGHT ON HEALTH AND THE BODY

The body is the servant of the mind. It obeys the operations of the mind, whether they be deliberately chosen or automatically expressed. At the bidding of unlawful thoughts the body sinks rapidly into disease and decay; at the command of glad and beautiful thoughts it becomes clothed with youthfulness and beauty.

Disease and health, like circumstances, are rooted in thought. Sickly thoughts will express themselves through a sickly body. Thoughts of fear have been known to kill a man as speedily as a bullet, and they are continually killing thousands of people just as surely though less rapidly. The people who live in fear of disease are the people who get it. Anxiety quickly demoralizes the whole body, and lays it open to the entrance of disease; while impure thoughts, even if not physically indulged, will soon shatter the nervous system.

Strong, pure, and happy thoughts build up the body in vigor and grace. The body is a delicate and plastic instrument, which responds readily to the thoughts by which it is impressed, and habits of thought will produce their own effects, good or bad, upon it.

Men will continue to have impure and poisoned blood so long as they propagate unclean thoughts. Out of a clean heart comes a clean life and a clean body. Out of a defiled mind proceeds a defiled life and corrupt body. Thought is the fountain of action, life and manifestation; make the fountain pure, and all will be pure.

Change of diet will not help a man who will not change his thoughts. When a man makes his thoughts pure, he no longer desires impure food.

If you would perfect your body, guard your mind. If you would renew your body, beautify your mind. Thoughts of malice, envy, disappointment, despondency, rob the body of its health and grace. A sour face does not come by chance; it is made by sour thoughts. Wrinkles that mar are drawn by folly, passion, pride.

I know a woman of ninety-six who has the bright, innocent face of a girl. I know a man well under middle age whose face is drawn into inharmonious contours. The one is the result of a sweet and sunny disposition; the other is the outcome of passion and discontent.

As you cannot have a sweet and wholesome abode unless you admit the air and sunshine freely into your rooms, so a strong body and a bright, happy, or serene countenance can only result from the free admittance into the mind of thoughts of joy and good will and serenity.

On the faces of the aged there are wrinkles made by sympathy, others by strong and pure thought, others are carved by passion. Who cannot distinguish them? With those who have lived righteously, age is calm, peaceful, and softly mellowed, like the setting sun. I have recently seen a philosopher on his deathbed. He was not old except in years. He died as sweetly and peacefully as he had lived.

There is no physician like cheerful thought for dissipating the ills of the body; there is no comforter to compare with good will for dispersing the shadows of grief and sorrow. To live continually in thoughts of ill will, cynicism, suspicion, and envy, is to be confined in a self-made prison hole. But to think well of all, to be cheerful with all, to patiently learn to find the good in all - such unselfish thoughts are the very portals of heaven; and to dwell day to day in thoughts of peace toward every creature will bring abounding peace to their possessor.

THOUGHT AND PURPOSE

Until thought is linked with purpose there is no intelligent accomplishment. With the majority the bark of thought is allowed to "drift" upon the ocean of life. Aimlessness is a vice, and such drifting must not continue for him who would steer clear of catastrophe and destruction.

They who have no central purpose in their life fall an easy prey to worries, fears, troubles, and self-pityings, all of which are indications of weakness, which lead, just as surely as deliberately planned sins (though by a different route), to failure, unhappiness, and loss, for weakness cannot persist in a power-evolving universe.

A man should conceive of a legitimate purpose in his heart, and set out to accomplish it. He should make this purpose the centralizing point of his thoughts. It may take the form of a spiritual ideal, or it may be a worldly object, according to his nature at the time being. But whichever it is, he should steadily focus his thought forces upon the object which he has set before him. He should make this purpose his supreme duty, and should devote himself to its attainment, not allowing his thoughts to wander away into ephemeral fancies, longings, and imaginings. This is the royal road to self-control and true concentration of thought. Even if he fails again and again to accomplish his purpose (as he necessarily must until weakness is overcome), the strength of character gained will be the measure of his true success, and this will form a new starting point for future power and triumph.

Those who are not prepared for the apprehension of a great purpose, should fix the thoughts upon the faultless performance of their duty, no matter how insignificant their task may appear. Only in this way can the thoughts be gathered and focused, and resolution and energy be developed, which being done, there is nothing which may not be accomplished.

The weakest soul, knowing its own weakness, and believing this truth - that strength can only be developed by effort and practice, will at once begin to exert itself, and adding effort to effort, patience to patience, and strength to strength, will never cease to develop, and will at last grow divinely strong.

As the physically weak man can make himself strong by careful and patient training, so the man of weak thoughts can make them strong by exercising himself in right thinking.

To put away aimlessness and weakness, and to begin to think with purpose, is to enter the ranks of those strong ones who only recognize failure as one of the pathways to attainment; who make all conditions serve them, and who think strongly, attempt fearlessly, and accomplish masterfully.

Having conceived of his purpose, a man should mentally mark out a straight pathway to its achievement, looking neither to the right nor to the left. Doubts and fears should be rigorously excluded; they are disintegrating elements which break up the straight line of effort, rendering it crooked, ineffectual, useless. Thoughts of doubt and fear never accomplish anything, and never can. They always lead to failure. Purpose, energy, power to do, and all strong thoughts cease when doubt and fear creep in.

The will to do springs from the knowledge that we can do. Doubt and fear are the great enemies of knowledge, and he who encourages them, who does not slay them, thwarts himself at every step.

He who has conquered doubt and fear has conquered failure. His every thought is allied with power, and all difficulties are bravely met and wisely overcome. His purposes are seasonably planted, and they bloom and bring forth fruit which does not fall prematurely to the ground.

Thought allied fearlessly to purpose becomes creative force. He who knows this is ready to become something higher and stronger than a mere bundle of wavering thoughts and fluctuating sensations. He who does this has become the conscious and intelligent wielder of his mental powers.

THE THOUGHT-FACTOR IN ACHIEVEMENT

All that a man achieves and all that he fails to achieve is the direct result of his own thoughts. In a justly ordered universe, where loss of equipoise would mean total destruction, individual responsibility must be absolute. A man's weakness and strength, purity and impurity, are his own, and not another man's. They are brought about by himself, and not by another; and they can only be altered by himself, never by another. His condition is also his own, and not another man's. His suffering and his happiness are evolved from within. As he thinks, so he is; as he continues to think, so he remains.

A strong man cannot help a weaker unless the weaker is willing to be helped, and even then the weak man must become strong of himself. He must, by his own efforts, develop the strength which he admires in another. None but himself can alter his condition.

It has been usual for men to think and to say, "Many men are slaves because one is an oppressor; let us hate the oppressor." Now however, there is among an increasing few a tendency to reverse this judgment, and to say, "One man is an oppressor because many are slaves; let us despise the slaves." The truth is that oppressor and slave are cooperators in ignorance, and, while seeming to afflict each other, are in reality afflicting themselves. A perfect Knowledge perceives the action of law in the weakness of the oppressed and the misapplied power of the oppressor. A perfect Love, seeing the suffering which both states entail, condemns neither. A perfect Compassion embraces both oppressor and oppressed.

He who has conquered weakness, and has put away all selfish thoughts, belongs neither to oppressor nor oppressed. He is free.

A man can only rise, conquer, and achieve by lifting up his thoughts. He can only remain weak, and abject, and miserable by refusing to lift up his thoughts.

Before a man can achieve anything, even in worldly things, he must lift his thoughts above slavish animal indulgence. He may not, in order to succeed, give up all animality and selfishness, by any means; but a portion of it must, at least, be sacrificed. A man whose first thought is bestial indulgence could neither think clearly nor plan methodically. He could not find and develop his latent resources, and would fail in any undertaking. Not having commenced manfully to control his thoughts, he is not in a position to control affairs and to adopt serious responsibilities. He is not fit to act independently and stand alone, but he is limited only by the thoughts which he chooses.

There can be no progress, no achievement without sacrifice. A man's worldly success will be in the measure that he sacrifices his confused animal thoughts, and fixes his mind on the development of his plans, and the strengthening of his resolution and self-reliance. And the higher he lifts his thoughts, the more manly, upright, and righteous he becomes, the greater will be his success, the more blessed an enduring will be his achievements.

The universe does not favor the greedy, the dishonest, the vicious, although on the mere surface it may sometimes appear to do so; it helps the honest, the magnanimous, the virtuous. All the great Teachers of the ages have declared this in varying forms, and to prove and know it a man has but to persist in making himself more and more virtuous by lifting up his thoughts.

Intellectual achievements are the result of thought consecrated to the search for knowledge, or for the beautiful and true in life and nature. Such achievements may be sometimes connected with vanity and ambition but they are not the outcome of those characteristics. They are the natural outgrowth of long an arduous effort, and of pure and unselfish thoughts.

Spiritual achievements are the consummation of holy aspirations. He who lives constantly in the conception of noble and lofty thoughts, who dwells upon all that is pure and unselfish, will, as surely as the sun reaches its zenith and the moon its full, become wise and noble in character, and rise into a position of influence and blessedness.

Achievement, of whatever kind, is the crown of effort, the diadem of thought. By the aid of self-control, resolution, purity, righteousness, and well-directed thought a man ascends. By the aid of animality, indolence, impurity, corruption, and confusion of thought a man descends.

A man may rise to high success in the world, and even to lofty altitudes in the spiritual realm, and again descend into weakness and wretchedness by allowing arrogant, selfish, and corrupt thoughts to take possession of him.

Victories attained by right thought can only be maintained by watchfulness. Many give way when success is assured, and rapidly fall back into failure.

All achievements, whether in the business, intellectual, or spiritual world, are the result of definitely directed thought, are governed by the same law and are of the same method; the only difference lies in the object of attainment.

He who would accomplish little must sacrifice little. He who would achieve much must sacrifice much. He who would attain highly must sacrifice greatly.

VISIONS AND IDEALS

The dreamers are the saviors of the world. As the visible world is sustained by the invisible, so men, through all their trials and sins and sordid vocations, are nourished by the beautiful visions of their solitary dreamers. Humanity cannot forget its dreamers. It cannot let their ideals fade and die. It lives in them. It knows them in the realities which it shall one day see and know.

Composer, sculptor, painter, poet, prophet, sage, these are the makers of the afterworld, the architects of heaven. The world is beautiful because they have lived; without them, laboring humanity would perish.

He who cherishes a beautiful vision, a lofty ideal in his heart, will one day realize it. Columbus cherished a vision of another world, and he discovered it. Copernicus fostered the vision of a multiplicity of worlds and a wider universe, and he revealed it. Buddha beheld the vision of a spiritual world of stainless beauty and perfect peace, and he entered into it.

Cherish your visions. Cherish your ideals. Cherish the music that stirs in your heart, the beauty that forms in your mind, the loveliness that drapes your purest thoughts, for out of them will grow all delightful conditions, all heavenly environment; of these, if you but remain true to them, your world will at last be built.

To desire is to obtain; to aspire is to achieve. Shall man's basest desires receive the fullest measure of gratification, and his purest aspirations starve for lack of sustenance? Such is not the Law. Such a condition of things can never obtain - "Ask and receive."

Dream lofty dreams, and as you dream, so shall you become. Your Vision is the promise of what you shall one day be. Your Ideal is the prophecy of what you shall at last unveil.

The greatest achievement was at first and for a time a dream. The oak sleeps in the acorn; the bird waits in the egg; and in the highest vision of the soul a waking angel stirs. Dreams are the seedlings of realities.

Your circumstances may be uncongenial, but they shall not long remain so if you but perceive an Ideal and strive to reach it. You cannot travel within and stand still without. Here is a youth hard pressed by poverty and labor; confined long hours in an unhealthy workshop; unschooled, and lacking all the arts of refinement. But he dreams of better things. He thinks of intelligence, of refinement, of grace and beauty. He conceives of, mentally builds up, an ideal condition of life. The vision of the wider liberty and a larger scope takes possession of him; unrest urges him to action, and he utilizes all his spare time and means, small though they are, to the development of his latent powers and resources.

Very soon so altered has his mind become that the workshop can no longer hold him. It has become so out of harmony with his mentality that it falls out of his life as a garment is cast aside, and with the growth of opportunities which fit the scope of his expanding powers, he passes out of it forever.

Years later we see this youth as a full-grown man. We find him a master of certain forces of the mind which he wields with world-wide influence and almost unequaled power. In his hands he holds the cords of gigantic responsibilities. He speaks, and lo! Lives are changed. Men and women hang upon his words and remold their characters, and, sunlike, he becomes the fixed and luminous center around which innumerable destinies revolve. He has realized the Vision of his youth. He has become one with his Ideal.

And you, too, youthful reader, will realize the Vision (not the idle wish) of your heart, be it base or beautiful, or a mixture of both, for you will always gravitate toward that which you secretly most love. Into your hands will be placed the exact results of your own thoughts; you will receive that which you earn, no more, no less. Whatever your present environment may be, you will fall, remain, or rise with your thoughts, your Vision, your Ideal. You will become as small as your controlling desire, as great as your dominant aspiration.

In the beautiful words of Stanton Kirkham Dave, "You may be keeping accounts, and presently you shall walk out of the door that for so long has seemed to you the barrier of your ideals, and shall find yourself before an audience - the pen still behind your ear, the ink stains on your fingers - and then and there shall pour out the torrent of your inspiration. You may be driving sheep, and you shall wander to the city - bucolic and open mouthed; shall wander under the intrepid guidance of the spirit into the studio of the master, and after a time he shall say, 'I have nothing more to teach you.' And now you have become the master, who did so recently dream of great things while driving sheep. You shall lay down the saw and the plane to take upon yourself the regeneration of the world."

The thoughtless, the ignorant, and the indolent, seeing only the apparent effects of things and not the things themselves, talk of luck, of fortune, and chance. See a man grow rich, they say, "How lucky he is!" Observing another become intellectual, they exclaim, "How highly favored he is!" And noting the saintly character and wide influence of another, the remark, "How chance aids him at every turn!"

They do not see the trials and failures and struggles which these men have voluntarily encountered in order to gain their experience. They have no knowledge of the sacrifices they have made, of the undaunted efforts they have put forth, of the faith they have exercised, that they might overcome the apparently insurmountable, and realize the Vision of their heart. They do not know the darkness and the heartaches; they only see the light and joy, and call it "luck"; do not see the long and arduous journey, but only behold the pleasant goal, and call it "good fortune"; do not understand the process, but only perceive the result, and call it "chance."

In all human affairs there are efforts, and there are results, and the strength of the effort is the measure of the result. Chance is not. "Gifts," powers, material, intellectual, and spiritual possessions are the fruits of effort. They are thoughts completed, objects accomplished, visions realized.

The vision that you glorify in your mind, the Ideal that you enthrone in your heart - this you will build your life by, this you will become.

SERENITY

Calmness of mind is one of the beautiful jewels of wisdom. It is the result of long and patient effort in self-control. Its presence is an indication of ripened experience, and of a more than ordinary knowledge of the laws and operations of thought.

A man becomes calm in the measure that he understands himself as a thought-evolved being, for such knowledge necessitates the understanding of others as the result of thought. As he develops a right understanding, and sees more and more clearly the internal relations of things by the action of cause and effect, he ceases to fuss and fume and worry and grieve, and remains poised, steadfast, serene.

The calm man, having learned how to govern himself, knows how to adapt himself to others; and they, in turn, reverence his spiritual strength, and feel that they can learn of him and rely upon him. The more tranquil a man becomes, the greater is his success, his influence, his power for good. Even the ordinary trader will find his business prosperity increase as he develops a greater self-control and equanimity, for people will always prefer to deal with a man whose demeanor is strongly equable.

The strong calm man is always loved and revered. He is like a shade-giving tree in a thirsty land, or a sheltering rock in a storm. Who does not love a tranquil heart, a sweet-tempered, balanced life? It does not matter whether it rains or shines, or what changes come to those possessing these blessings, for they are always sweet, serene, and calm. That exquisite poise of character which we call serenity is the last lesson culture; it is the flowering of life, the fruitage of the soul. It is precious as wisdom, more to be desired than gold - yea, than even fine gold. How insignificant mere money-seeking looks in comparison with a serene life - a life that dwells in the ocean of Truth, beneath the waves, beyond the reach of tempests, in the Eternal Calm!

How many people we know who sour their lives, who ruin all that is sweet and beautiful by explosive tempers, who destroy their poise of character, and make bad blood! It is a question whether the great majority of people do not ruin their lives and mar their happiness by lack of self-control. How few people we meet in life who are well-balanced, who have that exquisite poise which is characteristic of the finished character!

Yes, humanity surges with uncontrolled passion, is tumultuous with ungoverned grief, is blown about by anxiety and doubt. Only the wise man, only he whose thoughts are controlled and purified, makes the winds and the storms of the soul obey him.

Tempest tossed souls, wherever ye may be, under whatsoever conditions ye may live, know this - in the ocean of life the isles of Blessedness are smiling, and sunny shore of your ideal awaits your coming. Keep your hand firmly upon the helm of thought. In the bark of your soul reclines the commanding Master; He does but sleep; wake Him. Self-control is strength; Right Thought is mastery; Calmness is power.

Say unto your heart, "Peace, be still!"

THE END.

How to Live on 24 Hours a Day

by Arnold Bennett

TABLE OF CONTENTS

Chapter I

The Daily Miracle

Yes, he's one of those men that don't know how to manage. Good situation. Regular income. Quite enough for luxuries as well as needs. Not really extravagant. And yet the fellow's always in difficulties. Somehow he gets nothing out of his money. Excellent flat--half empty! Always looks as if he'd had the brokers in. New suit--old hat! Magnificent necktie--baggy trousers! Asks you to dinner: Cut glass--bad mutton, or Turkish coffee--cracked cup! He can't understand it. Explanation simply is that he fritters his income away. Wish I had the half of it! I'd show him--"

So we have most of us criticized, at one time or another, in our superior way.

We are nearly all chancellors of the exchequer: it is the pride of the moment. Newspapers are full of articles explaining how to live on such-and-such a sum, and these articles provoke a correspondence whose violence proves the interest they excite. Recently, in a daily organ, a battle raged round the question whether a woman can exist nicely in the country on L85 a year. I have seen an essay, "How to live on eight shillings a week." But I have never seen an essay, "How to live on twenty-four hours a day." Yet it has been said that time is money. That proverb understates the case. Time is a great deal more than money. If you have time you can obtain money--usually. But though you have the wealth of a cloakroom attendant at the Carlton Hotel, you cannot buy yourself a minute more time than I have, or the cat by the fire has.

Philosophers have explained space. They have not explained time. It is the inexplicable raw material of everything. With it, all is possible; without it, nothing. The supply of time is truly a daily miracle, an affair genuinely astonishing when one examines it. You wake up in the morning, and lo! Your purse is magically filled with twenty-four hours of the unmanufactured tissue of the universe of your life! It is yours. It is the most precious of possessions. A highly singular commodity, showered upon you in a manner as singular as the commodity itself!

For remark! No one can take it from you. It is unstealable. And no one receives either more or less than you receive.

Talk about an ideal democracy! In the realm of time there is no aristocracy of wealth, and no aristocracy of intellect. Genius is never rewarded by even an extra hour a day. And there is no punishment. Waste your infinitely precious commodity as much as you will, and the supply will never be withheld from you. No mysterious power will say:--"This man is a fool, if not a knave. He does not deserve time; he shall be cut off at the meter." It is more certain than consols, and payment of income is not affected by Sundays. Moreover, you cannot draw on the future. Impossible to get into debt! You can only waste the passing moment. You cannot waste tomorrow; it is kept for you. You cannot waste the next hour; it is kept for you.

I said the affair was a miracle. Is it not?

You have to live on this twenty-four hours of daily time. Out of it you have to spin health, pleasure, money, content, respect, and the evolution of your immortal soul. Its right use, its most effective use, is a matter of the highest urgency and of the most thrilling actuality. All depends on that. Your happiness--the elusive prize that you are all clutching for, my friends!--

85

depends on that. Strange that the newspapers, so enterprising and up-to-date as they are, are not full of "How to live on a given income of time," instead of "How to live on a given income of money"! Money is far commoner than time. When one reflects, one perceives that money is just about the commonest thing there is. It encumbers the earth in gross heaps.

If one can't contrive to live on a certain income of money, one earns a little more--or steals it, or advertises for it. One doesn't necessarily muddle one's life because one can't quite manage on a thousand pounds a year; one braces the muscles and makes it guineas, and balances the budget. But if one cannot arrange that an income of twenty-four hours a day shall exactly cover all proper items of expenditure, one does muddle one's life definitely. The supply of time, though gloriously regular, is cruelly restricted.

Which of us lives on twenty-four hours a day? And when I say "lives," I do not mean exists, nor "muddles through." Which of us is free from that uneasy feeling that the "great spending departments" of his daily life are not managed as they ought to be? Which of us is quite sure that his fine suit is not surmounted by a shameful hat, or that in attending to the crockery he has forgotten the quality of the food? Which of us is not saying to himself--which of us has not been saying to himself all his life: "I shall alter that when I have a little more time"?

We never shall have any more time. We have, and we have always had, all the time there is. It is the realisation of this profound and neglected truth (which, by the way, I have not discovered) that has led me to the minute practical examination of daily time-expenditure.

Chapter II

The Desire to Exceed One's Programme

"But," someone may remark, with the English disregard of everything except the point, "what is he driving at with his twenty-four hours a day? I have no difficulty in living on twenty-four hours a day. I do all that I want to do, and still find time to go in for newspaper competitions. Surely it is a simple affair, knowing that one has only twenty-four hours a day, to content one's self with twenty-four hours a day!"

To you, my dear sir, I present my excuses and apologies. You are precisely the man that I have been wishing to meet for about forty years. Will you kindly send me your name and address, and state your charge for telling me how you do it? Instead of me talking to you, you ought to be talking to me. Please come forward. That you exist, I am convinced, and that I have not yet encountered you is my loss. Meanwhile, until you appear, I will continue to chat with my companions in distress--that innumerable band of souls who are haunted, more or less painfully, by the feeling that the years slip by, and slip by, and slip by, and that they have not yet been able to get their lives into proper working order.

If we analyse that feeling, we shall perceive it to be, primarily, one of uneasiness, of expectation, of looking forward, of aspiration. It is a source of constant discomfort, for it behaves like a skeleton at the feast of all our enjoyments. We go to the theatre and laugh; but between the acts it raises a skinny finger at us. We rush violently for the last train, and while we are cooling a long age on the platform waiting for the last train, it promenades its bones up and down by our side and inquires: "O man, what hast thou done with thy youth? What art thou doing with thine age?" You may urge that this feeling of continuous looking forward, of aspiration, is part of life itself, and inseparable from life itself. True!

But there are degrees. A man may desire to go to Mecca. His conscience tells him that he ought to go to Mecca. He fares forth, either by the aid of Cook's, or unassisted; he may probably never reach Mecca; he may drown before he gets to Port Said; he may perish ingloriously on the coast of the Red Sea; his desire may remain eternally frustrate. Unfulfilled aspiration may always trouble him. But he will not be tormented in the same way as the man who, desiring to reach Mecca, and harried by the desire to reach Mecca, never leaves Brixton.

It is something to have left Brixton. Most of us have not left Brixton. We have not even taken a cab to Ludgate Circus and inquired from Cook's the price of a conducted tour. And our excuse to ourselves is that there are only twenty-four hours in the day.

If we further analyse our vague, uneasy aspiration, we shall, I think, see that it springs from a fixed idea that we ought to do something in addition to those things which we are loyally and morally obliged to do. We are obliged, by various codes written and unwritten, to maintain ourselves and our families (if any) in health and comfort, to pay our debts, to save, to increase our prosperity by increasing our efficiency. A task sufficiently difficult! A task which very few of us achieve! A task often beyond our skill! Yet, if we succeed in it, as we sometimes do, we are not satisfied; the skeleton is still with us.

And even when we realise that the task is beyond our skill, that our powers cannot cope with it, we feel that we should be less discontented if we gave to our powers, already overtaxed, something still further to do.

And such is, indeed, the fact. The wish to accomplish something outside their formal programme is common to all men who in the course of evolution have risen past a certain level.

Until an effort is made to satisfy that wish, the sense of uneasy waiting for something to start which has not started will remain to disturb the peace of the soul. That wish has been called by many names. It is one form of the universal desire for knowledge. And it is so strong that men whose whole lives have been given to the systematic acquirement of knowledge have been driven by it to overstep the limits of their programme in search of still more knowledge. Even Herbert Spencer, in my opinion the greatest mind that ever lived, was often forced by it into agreeable little backwaters of inquiry.

I imagine that in the majority of people who are conscious of the wish to live--that is to say, people who have intellectual curiosity--the aspiration to exceed formal programmes takes a literary shape. They would like to embark on a course of reading. Decidedly the British people are becoming more and more literary. But I would point out that literature by no means comprises the whole field of knowledge, and that the disturbing thirst to improve one's self--to increase one's knowledge--may well be slaked quite apart from literature. With the various ways of slaking I shall deal later. Here I merely point out to those who have no natural sympathy with literature that literature is not the only well.

Chapter III

Precautions Before Beginning

Now that I have succeeded (if succeeded I have) in persuading you to admit to yourself that you are constantly haunted by a suppressed dissatisfaction with your own arrangement of your daily life; and that the primal cause of that inconvenient dissatisfaction is the feeling that you are every day leaving undone something which you would like to do, and which, indeed, you are always hoping to do when you have "more time"; and now that I have drawn your attention to the glaring, dazzling truth that you never will have "more time," since you already have all the time there is--you expect me to let you into some wonderful secret by which you may at any rate approach the ideal of a perfect arrangement of the day, and by which, therefore, that haunting, unpleasant, daily disappointment of things left undone will be got rid of!

I have found no such wonderful secret. Nor do I expect to find it, nor do I expect that anyone else will ever find it. It is undiscovered. When you first began to gather my drift, perhaps there was a resurrection of hope in your breast. Perhaps you said to yourself, "This man will show me an easy, unfatiguing way of doing what I have so long in vain wished to do." Alas, no! The fact is that there is no easy way, no royal road. The path to Mecca is extremely hard and stony, and the worst of it is that you never quite get there after all.

The most important preliminary to the task of arranging one's life so that one may live fully and comfortably within one's daily budget of twenty-four hours is the calm realisation of the extreme difficulty of the task, of the sacrifices and the endless effort which it demands. I cannot too strongly insist on this.

If you imagine that you will be able to achieve your ideal by ingeniously planning out a time-table with a pen on a piece of paper, you had better give up hope at once. If you are not prepared for discouragements and disillusions; if you will not be content with a small result for a big effort, then do not begin. Lie down again and resume the uneasy doze which you call your existence.

It is very sad, is it not, very depressing and sombre? And yet I think it is rather fine, too, this necessity for the tense bracing of the will before anything worth doing can be done. I rather like it myself. I feel it to be the chief thing that differentiates me from the cat by the fire.

"Well," you say, "assume that I am braced for the battle. Assume that I have carefully weighed and comprehended your ponderous remarks; how do I begin?" Dear sir, you simply begin. There is no magic method of beginning. If a man standing on the edge of a swimming bath and wanting to jump into the cold water should ask you, "How do I begin to jump?" you would merely reply, "Just jump. Take hold of your nerves, and jump."

As I have previously said, the chief beauty about the constant supply of time is that you cannot waste it in advance. The next year, the next day, the next hour are lying ready for you, as perfect, as unspoilt, as if you had never wasted or misapplied a single moment in all your career. Which fact is very gratifying and reassuring. You can turn over a new leaf every hour if you choose. Therefore no object is served in waiting till next week, or even until tomorrow. You may fancy that the water will be warmer next week. It won't. It will be colder.

But before you begin, let me murmur a few words of warning in your private ear.

Let me principally warn you against your own ardour. Ardour in well-doing is a misleading and a treacherous thing. It cries out loudly for employment. You can't satisfy it at first, it wants more and more. It is eager to move mountains and divert the course of rivers. It isn't content till it perspires. And then, too often, when it feels the perspiration on its brow, it wearies all of a sudden and dies, without even putting itself to the trouble of saying, "I've had enough of this."

Beware of undertaking too much at the start. Be content with quite a little. Allow for accidents. Allow for human nature, especially your own.

A failure or so, in itself, would not matter, if it did not incur a loss of self-esteem and of self-confidence. But just as nothing succeeds like success, so nothing fails like failure. Most people who are ruined are ruined by attempting too much. Therefore, in setting out on the immense enterprise of living fully and comfortably within the narrow limits of twenty-four hours a day, let us avoid at any cost the risk of an early failure. I will not agree that, in this business at any rate, a glorious failure is better than a petty success. I am all for the petty success. A glorious failure leads to nothing; a petty success may lead to a success that is not petty.

So let us begin to examine the budget of the day's time. You say your day is already full to overflowing. How? You actually spend in earning your livelihood--how much? Seven hours, on the average? And in actual sleep, seven? I will add two hours, and be generous. And I will defy you to account to me on the spur of the moment for the other eight hours.

Chapter IV

The Cause of the Troubles

In order to come to grips at once with the question of time-expenditure in all its actuality, I must choose an individual case for examination. I can only deal with one case, and that case cannot be the average case, because there is no such case as the average case, just as there is no such man as the average man. Every man and every man's case is special.

But if I take the case of a Londoner who works in an office, whose office hours are from ten to six, and who spends fifty minutes morning and night in travelling between his house door and his office door, I shall have got as near to the average as facts permit. There are men who have to work longer for a living, but there are others who do not have to work so long.

Fortunately the financial side of existence does not interest us here; for our present purpose the clerk at a pound a week is exactly as well off as the millionaire in Carlton House-terrace.

Now the great and profound mistake which my typical man makes in regard to his day is a mistake of general attitude, a mistake which vitiates and weakens two-thirds of his energies and interests. In the majority of instances he does not precisely feel a passion for his business - at best he does not dislike it. He begins his business functions with reluctance, as late as he can, and he ends them with joy, as early as he can. And his engines while he is engaged in his business are seldom at their full "h.p." (I know that I shall be accused by angry readers of traducing the city worker; but I am pretty thoroughly acquainted with the City, and I stick to what I say).

Yet in spite of all this he persists in looking upon those hours from ten to six as "the day," to which the ten hours preceding them and the six hours following them are nothing but a prologue and epilogue. Such an attitude, unconscious though it be, of course kills his interest in the odd sixteen hours, with the result that, even if he does not waste them, he does not count them; he regards them simply as margin.

This general attitude is utterly illogical and unhealthy, since it formally gives the central prominence to a patch of time and a bunch of activities which the man's one idea is to "get through" and have "done with." If a man makes two-thirds of his existence subservient to one-third, for which admittedly he has no absolutely feverish zest, how can he hope to live fully and completely? He cannot.

If my typical man wishes to live fully and completely he must, in his mind, arrange a day within a day. And this inner day, a Chinese box in a larger Chinese box, must begin at 6 p.m. and end at 10 a.m. It is a day of sixteen hours; and during all these sixteen hours he has nothing whatever to do but cultivate his body and his soul and his fellow men. During those sixteen hours he is free; he is not a wage-earner; he is not preoccupied with monetary cares; he is just as good as a man with a private income. This must be his attitude. And his attitude is all-important. His success in life (much more important than the amount of estate upon what his executors will have to pay estate duty) depends on it.

What? You say that full energy given to those sixteen hours will lessen the value of the business eight? Not so. On the contrary, it will assuredly increase the value of the business eight. One of the chief things which my typical man has to learn is that the mental faculties are capable of a continuous hard activity - they do not tire like an arm or a leg. All they want is change--not rest, except in sleep.

I shall now examine the typical man's current method of employing the sixteen hours that are entirely his, beginning with his uprising. I will merely indicate things which he does and which I think he ought not to do, postponing my suggestions for "planting" the times which I shall have cleared--as a settler clears spaces in a forest.

In justice to him I must say that he wastes very little time before he leaves the house in the morning at 9.10. In too many houses he gets up at nine, breakfasts between 9.7 and 9.9 1/2, and then bolts. But immediately as he bangs the front door his mental faculties, which are tireless, become idle. He walks to the station in a condition of mental coma. Arrived there, he usually has to wait for the train. On hundreds of suburban stations every morning you see men calmly strolling up and down platforms while railway companies unblushingly rob them of time, which is more than money. Hundreds of thousands of hours are thus lost every day simply because my typical man thinks so little of time that it has never occurred to him to take quite easy precautions against the risk of its loss.

He has a solid coin of time to spend every day--call it a sovereign. He must get change for it, and in getting change he is content to lose heavily.

Supposing that in selling him a ticket the company said, "We will change you a sovereign, but we shall charge you three halfpence for doing so," what would my typical man exclaim? Yet that is the equivalent of what the company does when it robs him of five minutes twice a day.

You say I am dealing with minutiae. I am. And later on I will justify myself.

Now will you kindly buy your paper and step into the train?

Chapter V

Tennis and the Immortal Soul

You get into the morning train with your newspaper, and you calmly and majestically give yourself up to your newspaper. You do not hurry. You know you have at least half an hour of security in front of you. As your glance lingers idly at the advertisements of shipping and of songs on the outer pages, your air is the air of a leisured man, wealthy in time, of a man from some planet where there are a hundred and twenty-four hours a day instead of twenty-four. I am an impassioned reader of newspapers. I read five English and two French dailies, and the newsagents alone know how many weeklies, regularly. I am obliged to mention this personal fact lest I should be accused of a prejudice against newspapers when I say that I object to the reading of newspapers in the morning train. Newspapers are produced with rapidity, to be read with rapidity. There is no place in my daily programme for newspapers. I read them as I may in odd moments. But I do read them. The idea of devoting to them thirty or forty consecutive minutes of wonderful solitude (for nowhere can one more perfectly immerse one's self in one's self than in a compartment full of silent, withdrawn, smoking males) is to me repugnant. I cannot possibly allow you to scatter priceless pearls of time with such Oriental lavishness. You are not the Shah of time. Let me respectfully remind you that you have no more time than I have. No newspaper reading in trains! I have already "put by" about three-quarters of an hour for use.

Now you reach your office. And I abandon you there till six o'clock. I am aware that you have nominally an hour (often in reality an hour and a half) in the midst of the day, less than half of which time is given to eating. But I will leave you all that to spend as you choose. You may read your newspapers then.

I meet you again as you emerge from your office. You are pale and tired. At any rate, your wife says you are pale, and you give her to understand that you are tired. During the journey home you have been gradually working up the tired feeling. The tired feeling hangs heavy over the mighty suburbs of London like a virtuous and melancholy cloud, particularly in winter. You don't eat immediately on your arrival home. But in about an hour or so you feel as if you could sit up and take a little nourishment. And you do. Then you smoke, seriously; you see friends; you potter; you play cards; you flirt with a book; you note that old age is creeping on; you take a stroll; you caress the piano.... By Jove! A quarter past eleven. You then devote quite forty minutes to thinking about going to bed; and it is conceivable that you are acquainted with a genuinely good whisky. At last you go to bed, exhausted by the day's work. Six hours, probably more, have gone since you left the office--gone like a dream, gone like magic, unaccountably gone!

That is a fair sample case. But you say: "It's all very well for you to talk. A man "is" tired. A man must see his friends. He can't always be on the stretch." Just so. But when you arrange to go to the theatre (especially with a pretty woman) what happens? You rush to the suburbs; you spare no toil to make yourself glorious in fine raiment; you rush back to town in another train; you keep yourself on the stretch for four hours, if not five; you take her home; you take yourself home. You don't spend three-quarters of an hour in "thinking about" going to bed. You go. Friends and fatigue have equally been forgotten, and the evening has seemed so exquisitely long (or perhaps too short)! And do you remember that time when you were persuaded to sing in the chorus of the amateur operatic society, and slaved two hours every other night for three months? Can you deny that when you have something definite to look forward to at eventide, something that is to employ all your energy--the thought of that something gives a glow and a more intense vitality to the whole day?

What I suggest is that at six o'clock you look facts in the face and admit that you are not tired (because you are not, you know), and that you arrange your evening so that it is not cut in the middle by a meal. By so doing you will have a clear expanse of at least three hours. I do not suggest that you should employ three hours every night of your life in using up your mental energy. But I do suggest that you might, for a commencement, employ an hour and a half every other evening in some important and consecutive cultivation of the mind. You will still be left with three evenings for friends, bridge, tennis, domestic scenes, odd reading, pipes, gardening, pottering, and prize competitions. You will still have the terrific wealth of forty-five hours between 2 p.m. Saturday and 10 a.m. Monday. If you persevere you will soon want to pass four evenings, and perhaps five, in some sustained endeavour to be genuinely alive. And you will fall out of that habit of muttering to yourself at 11.15 p.m., "Time to be thinking about going to bed." The man who begins to go to bed forty minutes before he opens his bedroom door is bored; that is to say, he is not living.

But remember, at the start, those ninety nocturnal minutes thrice a week must be the most important minutes in the ten thousand and eighty. They must be sacred, quite as sacred as a dramatic rehearsal or a tennis match. Instead of saying, "Sorry I can't see you, old chap, but I have to run off to the tennis club," you must say, "...but I have to work." This, I admit, is intensely difficult to say. Tennis is so much more urgent than the immortal soul.

Chapter VI

Remember Human Nature

I have incidentally mentioned the vast expanse of forty-four hours between leaving business at 2 p.m. on Saturday and returning to business at 10 a.m. on Monday. And here I must touch on the point whether the week should consist of six days or of seven. For many years--in fact, until I was approaching forty--my own week consisted of seven days. I was constantly being informed by older and wiser people that more work, more genuine living, could be got out of six days than out of seven.

And it is certainly true that now, with one day in seven in which I follow no programme and make no effort save what the caprice of the moment dictates, I appreciate intensely the moral value of a weekly rest. Nevertheless, had I my life to arrange over again, I would do again as I have done. Only those who have lived at the full stretch seven days a week for a long time can appreciate the full beauty of a regular recurring idleness. Moreover, I am ageing. And it is a question of age. In cases of abounding youth and exceptional energy and desire for effort I should say unhesitatingly: Keep going, day in, day out.

But in the average case I should say: Confine your formal programme (super-programme, I mean) to six days a week. If you find yourself wishing to extend it, extend it, but only in proportion to your wish; and count the time extra as a windfall, not as regular income, so that you can return to a six-day programme without the sensation of being poorer, of being a backslider.

Let us now see where we stand. So far we have marked for saving out of the waste of days, half an hour at least on six mornings a week, and one hour and a half on three evenings a week. Total, seven hours and a half a week.

I propose to be content with that seven hours and a half for the present. "What?" you cry. "You pretend to show us how to live, and you only deal with seven hours and a half out of a hundred and sixty-eight! Are you going to perform a miracle with your seven hours and a half?" Well, not to mince the matter, I am--if you will kindly let me! That is to say, I am going to ask you to attempt an experience which, while perfectly natural and explicable, has all the air of a miracle. My contention is that the full use of those seven-and-a-half hours will quicken the whole life of the week, add zest to it, and increase the interest which you feel in even the most banal occupations. You practise physical exercises for a mere ten minutes morning and evening, and yet you are not astonished when your physical health and strength are beneficially affected every hour of the day, and your whole physical outlook changed. Why should you be astonished that an average of over an hour a day given to the mind should permanently and completely enliven the whole activity of the mind?

More time might assuredly be given to the cultivation of one's self. And in proportion as the time was longer the results would be greater. But I prefer to begin with what looks like a trifling effort.

It is not really a trifling effort, as those will discover who have yet to essay it. To "clear" even seven hours and a half from the jungle is passably difficult. For some sacrifice has to be made. One may have spent one's time badly, but one did spend it, one did do something with it, however ill advised that something may have been. To do something else means a change of habits.

And habits are the very dickens to change! Further, any change, even a change for the better, is always accompanied by drawbacks and discomforts. If you imagine that you will be able to devote seven hours and a half a week to serious, continuous effort, and still live your old life, you are mistaken. I repeat that some sacrifice, and an immense deal of volition, will be necessary. And it is because I know the difficulty, it is because I know the almost disastrous effect of failure in such an enterprise, that I earnestly advise a very humble beginning. You must safeguard your self-respect. Self-respect is at the root of all purposefulness, and a failure in an enterprise deliberately planned deals a desperate wound at one's self-respect. Hence I iterate and reiterate: Start quietly, unostentatiously.

When you have conscientiously given seven hours and a half a week to the cultivation of your vitality for three months--then you may begin to sing louder and tell yourself what wondrous things you are capable of doing.

Before coming to the method of using the indicated hours, I have one final suggestion to make. That is, as regards the evenings, to allow much more than an hour and a half in which to do the work of an hour and a half. Remember the chance of accidents. Remember human nature. And give yourself, say, from 9 to 11.30 for your task of ninety minutes.

Chapter VII

Controlling the Mind

People say: "One can't help one's thoughts." But one can. The control of the thinking machine is perfectly possible. And since nothing whatever happens to us outside our own brain, since nothing hurts us or gives us pleasure except within the brain, the supreme importance of being able to control what goes on in that mysterious brain is patent. This idea is one of the oldest platitudes, but it is a platitude who's profound truth and urgency most people live and die without realising. People complain of the lack of power to concentrate, not witting that they may acquire the power, if they choose.

And without the power to concentrate--that is to say, without the power to dictate to the brain its task and to ensure obedience--true life is impossible. Mind control is the first element of a full existence.

Hence, it seems to me, the first business of the day should be to put the mind through its paces. You look after your body, inside and out; you run grave danger in hacking hairs off your skin; you employ a whole army of individuals, from the milkman to the pig-killer, to enable you to bribe your stomach into decent behaviour. Why not devote a little attention to the far more delicate machinery of the mind, especially as you will require no extraneous aid? It is for this portion of the art and craft of living that I have reserved the time from the moment of quitting your door to the moment of arriving at your office.

"What? I am to cultivate my mind in the street, on the platform, in the train, and in the crowded street again?" Precisely. Nothing simpler! No tools required! Not even a book. Nevertheless, the affair is not easy.

When you leave your house, concentrate your mind on a subject (no matter what, to begin with). You will not have gone ten yards before your mind has skipped away under your very eyes and is larking round the corner with another subject.

Bring it back by the scruff of the neck. Ere you have reached the station you will have brought it back about forty times. Do not despair. Continue. Keep it up. You will succeed. You cannot by any chance fail if you persevere. It is idle to pretend that your mind is incapable of concentration. Do you not remember that morning when you received a disquieting letter which demanded a very carefully-worded answer? How you kept your mind steadily on the subject of the answer, without a second's intermission, until you reached your office; whereupon you instantly sat down and wrote the answer? That was a case in which *you* were roused by circumstances to such a degree of vitality that you were able to dominate your mind like a tyrant. You would have no trifling. You insisted that its work should be done, and its work was done.

By the regular practice of concentration (as to which there is no secret--save the secret of perseverance) you can tyrannise over your mind (which is not the highest part of *you*) every hour of the day, and in no matter what place. The exercise is a very convenient one. If you got into your morning train with a pair of dumb-bells for your muscles or an encyclopaedia in ten volumes for your learning, you would probably excite remark. But as you walk in the street, or sit in the corner of the compartment behind a pipe, or "strap-hang" on the Subterranean, who is to know that you are engaged in the most important of daily acts? What asinine boor can laugh at you?

I do not care what you concentrate on, so long as you concentrate. It is the mere disciplining of the thinking machine that counts. But still, you may as well kill two birds with one stone, and concentrate on something useful. I suggest--it is only a suggestion--a little chapter of Marcus Aurelius or Epictetus.

Do not, I beg, shy at their names. For myself, I know nothing more "actual," more bursting with plain common-sense, applicable to the daily life of plain persons like you and me (who hate airs, pose, and nonsense) than Marcus Aurelius or Epictetus. Read a chapter--and so short they are, the chapters! --in the evening and concentrate on it the next morning. You will see.

Yes, my friend, it is useless for you to try to disguise the fact. I can hear your brain like a telephone at my ear. You are saying to yourself: "This fellow was doing pretty well up to his seventh chapter. He had begun to interest me faintly. But what he says about thinking in trains, and concentration, and so on, is not for me. It may be well enough for some folks, but it isn't in my line."

It is for you, I passionately repeat; it is for you. Indeed, you are the very man I am aiming at.

Throw away the suggestion, and you throw away the most precious suggestion that was ever offered to you. It is not my suggestion. It is the suggestion of the most sensible, practical, hard-headed men who have walked the earth. I only give it you at second-hand. Try it. Get your mind in hand. And see how the process cures half the evils of life --especially worry, that miserable, avoidable, shameful disease--worry!

Chapter VIII

The Reflective Mood

The exercise of concentrating the mind (to which at least half an hour a day should be given) is a mere preliminary, like scales on the piano. Having acquired power over that most unruly member of one's complex organism, one has naturally to put it to the yoke. Useless to possess an obedient mind unless one profits to the furthest possible degree by its obedience. A prolonged primary course of study is indicated.

Now as to what this course of study should be there cannot be any question; there never has been any question. All the sensible people of all ages are agreed upon it. And it is not literature, nor is it any other art, nor is it history, nor is it any science. It is the study of one's self. Man, know thyself. These words are so hackneyed that verily I blush to write them. Yet they must be written, for they need to be written. (I take back my blush, being ashamed of it.) Man, know thyself. I say it out loud. The phrase is one of those phrases with which everyone is familiar, of which everyone acknowledges the value, and which only the most sagacious put into practice. I don't know why. I am entirely convinced that what is more than anything else lacking in the life of the average well-intentioned man of today is the reflective mood.

We do not reflect. I mean that we do not reflect upon genuinely important things; upon the problem of our happiness, upon the main direction in which we are going, upon what life is giving to us, upon the share which reason has (or has not) in determining our actions, and upon the relation between our principles and our conduct.

And yet you are in search of happiness, are you not? Have you discovered it?

The chances are that you have not. The chances are that you have already come to believe that happiness is unattainable. But men have attained it. And they have attained it by realising that happiness does not spring from the procuring of physical or mental pleasure, but from the development of reason and the adjustment of conduct to principles.

I suppose that you will not have the audacity to deny this. And if you admit it, and still devote no part of your day to the deliberate consideration of your reason, principles, and conduct, you admit also that while striving for a certain thing you are regularly leaving undone the one act which is necessary to the attainment of that thing.

Now, shall I blush, or will you?

Do not fear that I mean to thrust certain principles upon your attention. I care not (in this place) what your principles are. Your principles may induce you to believe in the righteousness of burglary. I don't mind. All I urge is that a life in which conduct does not fairly well accord with principles is a silly life; and that conduct can only be made to accord with principles by means of daily examination, reflection, and resolution. What leads to the permanent sorrowfulness of burglars is that their principles are contrary to burglary. If they genuinely believed in the moral excellence of burglary, penal servitude would simply mean so many happy years for them; all martyrs are happy years for them; all martyrs are happy, because their conduct and their principles agree.

As for reason (which makes conduct, and is not unconnected with the making of principles), it plays a far smaller part in our lives than we fancy. We are supposed to be reasonable but we are much more instinctive than reasonable. And the less we reflect, the less reasonable we shall be. The next time you get cross with the waiter because your steak is over-cooked, ask reason to step into the cabinet-room of your mind, and consult her. She will probably tell you that the waiter did not cook the steak, and had no control over the cooking of the steak; and that even if he alone was to blame, you accomplished nothing good by getting cross; you merely lost your dignity, looked a fool in the eyes of sensible men, and soured the waiter, while producing no effect whatever on the steak.

The result of this consultation with reason (for which she makes no charge) will be that when once more your steak is over-cooked you will treat the waiter as a fellow-creature, remain quite calm in a kindly spirit, and politely insist on having a fresh steak. The gain will be obvious and solid.

In the formation or modification of principles, and the practice of conduct, much help can be derived from printed books (issued at sixpence each and upwards). I mentioned in my last chapter Marcus Aurelius and Epictetus. Certain even more widely known works will occur at once to the memory. I may also mention Pascal, La Bruyere, and Emerson. For myself, you do not catch me travelling without my Marcus Aurelius. Yes, books are valuable. But not reading of books will take the place of a daily, candid, honest examination of what one has recently done, and what one is about to do--of a steady looking at one's self in the face (disconcerting though the sight may be).

When shall this important business be accomplished? The solitude of the evening journey home appears to me to be suitable for it. A reflective mood naturally follows the exertion of having earned the day's living. Of course if, instead of attending to an elementary and profoundly important duty, you prefer to read the paper (which you might just as well read while waiting for your dinner) I have nothing to say. But attend to it at some time of the day you must. I now come to the evening hours.

Chapter IX

Interest in the Arts

Many people pursue a regular and uninterrupted course of idleness in the evenings because they think that there is no alternative to idleness but the study of literature; and they do not happen to have a taste for literature. This is a great mistake.

Of course it is impossible, or at any rate very difficult, properly to study anything whatever without the aid of printed books. But if you desire to understand the deeper depths of bridge or of boat sailing you would not be deterred by your lack of interest in literature from reading the best books on bridge or boat sailing. We must, therefore, distinguish between literature, and books treating of subjects not literary. I shall come to literature in due course.

Let me now remark to those who have never read Meredith, and who are capable of being unmoved by a discussion as to whether Mr. Stephen Phillips is or is not a true poet, that they are perfectly within their rights. It is not a crime not to love literature. It is not a sign of imbecility. The mandarins of literature will order out to instant execution the unfortunate individual who does not comprehend, say, the influence of Wordsworth on Tennyson. But that is only their impudence. Where would they be, I wonder, if requested to explain the influences that went to make Tschaikowsky's "Pathetic Symphony"?

There are enormous fields of knowledge quite outside literature which will yield magnificent results to cultivators. For example (since I have just mentioned the most popular piece of high-class music in England to-day), I am reminded that the Promenade Concerts begin in August. You go to them. You smoke your cigar or cigarette (and I regret to say that you strike your matches during the soft bars of the "Lohengrin" overture), and you enjoy the music. But you say you cannot play the piano or the fiddle, or even the banjo; that you know nothing of music.

What does that matter? That you have a genuine taste for music is proved by the fact that, in order to fill his hall with you and your peers, the conductor is obliged to provide programmes from which bad music is almost entirely excluded (a change from the old Covent Garden days!).

Now surely your inability to perform "The Maiden's Prayer" on a piano need not prevent you from making yourself familiar with the construction of the orchestra to which you listen a couple of nights a week during a couple of months! As things are, you probably think of the orchestra as a heterogeneous mass of instruments producing a confused agreeable mass of sound. You do not listen for details because you have never trained your ears to listen to details.

If you were asked to name the instruments which play the great theme at the beginning of the C minor symphony you could not name them for your life's sake. Yet you admire the C minor symphony. It has thrilled you. It will thrill you again. You have even talked about it, in an expansive mood, to that lady--you know whom I mean. And all you can positively state about the C minor symphony is that Beethoven composed it and that it is a "jolly fine thing."

Now, if you have read, say, Mr. Krehbiel's "How to Listen to Music" (which can be got at any bookseller's for less than the price of a stall at the Alhambra, and which contains photographs of all the orchestral instruments and plans of the arrangement of orchestras) you would next go to a promenade concert with an astonishing intensification of interest in it. Instead of a confused mass, the orchestra would appear to you as what it is--a marvellously balanced organism whose various groups of members each have a different and an indispensable function. You would spy out the instruments, and listen for their respective sounds. You would know the gulf that separates a French horn from an English horn, and you would perceive why a player of the hautboy gets higher wages than a fiddler, though the fiddle is the more difficult instrument. You would *live* at a promenade concert, whereas previously you had merely existed there in a state of beatific coma, like a baby gazing at a bright object.

The foundations of a genuine, systematic knowledge of music might be laid. You might specialise your inquiries either on a particular form of music (such as the symphony), or on the works of a particular composer. At the end of a year of forty-eight weeks of three brief evenings each, combined with a study of programmes and attendances at concerts chosen out of your increasing knowledge, you would really know something about music, even though you were as far off as ever from jangling "The Maiden's Prayer" on the piano.

"But I hate music!" you say. My dear sir, I respect you.

What applies to music applies to the other arts. I might mention Mr. Clermont Witt's "How to Look at Pictures," or Mr. Russell Sturgis's "How to Judge Architecture," as beginnings (merely beginnings) of systematic vitalising knowledge in other arts, the materials for whose study abound in London.

"I hate all the arts!" you say. My dear sir, I respect you more and more.

I will deal with your case next, before coming to literature.

Chapter X

Nothing in Life Is Humdrum

Art is a great thing. But it is not the greatest. The most important of all perceptions is the continual perception of cause and effect-in other words, the perception of the continuous development of the universe in still other words, the perception of the course of evolution. When one has thoroughly got imbued into one's head the leading truth that nothing happens without a cause, one grows not only large-minded, but large-hearted.

It is hard to have one's watch stolen, but one reflects that the thief of the watch became a thief from causes of heredity and environment which are as interesting as they are scientifically comprehensible; and one buys another watch, if not with joy, at any rate with a philosophy that makes bitterness impossible. One loses, in the study of cause and effect, that absurd air which so many people have of being always shocked and pained by the curiousness of life. Such people live amid human nature as if human nature were a foreign country full of awful foreign customs. But, having reached maturity, one ought surely to be ashamed of being a stranger in a strange land!

The study of cause and effect, while it lessens the painfulness of life, adds to life's picturesqueness. The man to whom evolution is but a name looks at the sea as a grandiose, monotonous spectacle, which he can witness in August for three shillings third-class return. The man who is imbued with the idea of development, of continuous cause and effect, perceives in the sea an element which in the day-before-yesterday of geology was vapour, which yesterday was boiling, and which to-morrow will inevitably be ice.

He perceives that a liquid is merely something on its way to be solid, and he is penetrated by a sense of the tremendous, changeful picturesqueness of life. Nothing will afford a more durable satisfaction than the constantly cultivated appreciation of this. It is the end of all science.

Cause and effect are to be found everywhere. Rents went up in Shepherd's Bush. It was painful and shocking that rents should go up in Shepherd's Bush. But to a certain point we are all scientific students of cause and effect, and there was not a clerk lunching at a Lyons Restaurant who did not scientifically put two and two together and see in the (once) Two-penny Tube the cause of an excessive demand for wigwams in Shepherd's Bush, and in the excessive demand for wigwams the cause of the increase in the price of wigwams.

"Simple!" you say, disdainfully. Everything - the whole complex movement of the universe - is as simple as that, when you can sufficiently put two and two together. And, my dear sir, perhaps you happen to be an estate agent's clerk, and you hate the arts, and you want to foster your immortal soul, and you can't be interested in your business because it's so humdrum.

Nothing is humdrum.

The tremendous, changeful picturesqueness of life is marvellously shown in an estate agent's office. What! There was a block of traffic in Oxford Street. To avoid the block people actually began to travel under the cellars and drains, and the result was a rise of rents in Shepherd's Bush! And you say that isn't picturesque! Suppose you were to study, in this spirit, the property question in London for an hour and a half every other evening. Would it not give zest to your business, and transform your whole life?

You would arrive at more difficult problems. And you would be able to tell us why, as the natural result of cause and effect, the longest straight street in London is about a yard and a half in length, while the longest absolutely straight street in Paris extends for miles. I think you will admit that in an estate agent's clerk I have not chosen an example that specially favours my theories.

You are a bank clerk, and you have not read that breathless romance (disguised as a scientific study), Walter Bagehot's "Lombard Street"? Ah, my dear sir, if you had begun with that, and followed it up for ninety minutes every other evening, how enthralling your business would be to you, and how much more clearly you would understand human nature.

You are "penned in town," but you love excursions to the country and the observation of wild life - certainly a heart-enlarging diversion. Why don't you walk out of your house door, in your slippers, to the nearest gas lamp of a night with a butterfly net, and observe the wild life of common and rare moths that is beating about it, and co-ordinate the knowledge thus obtained and build a superstructure on it, and at last get to know something about something?

You need not be devoted to the arts, not to literature, in order to live fully.

The whole field of daily habit and scene is waiting to satisfy that curiosity which means life, and the satisfaction of which means an understanding heart.

I promised to deal with your case, O man who hates art and literature, and I have dealt with it. I now come to the case of the person, happily very common, who does "like reading."

Chapter XI

Serious Reading

Novels are excluded from "serious reading," so that the man who, bent on self-improvement, has been deciding to devote ninety minutes three times a week to a complete study of the works of Charles Dickens will be well advised to alter his plans. The reason is not that novels are not serious--some of the great literature of the world is in the form of prose fiction--the reason is that bad novels ought not to be read, and that good novels never demand any appreciable mental application on the part of the reader. It is only the bad parts of Meredith's novels that are difficult. A good novel rushes you forward like a skiff down a stream, and you arrive at the end, perhaps breathless, but unexhausted. The best novels involve the least strain. Now in the cultivation of the mind one of the most important factors is precisely the feeling of strain, of difficulty, of a task which one part of you is anxious to achieve and another part of you is anxious to shirk; and that f eeling cannot be got in facing a novel. You do not set your teeth in order to read "Anna Karenina." Therefore, though you should read novels, you should not read them in those ninety minutes.

Imaginative poetry produces a far greater mental strain than novels. It produces probably the severest strain of any form of literature. It is the highest form of literature. It yields the highest form of pleasure, and teaches the highest form of wisdom. In a word, there is nothing to compare with it. I say this with sad consciousness of the fact that the majority of people do not read poetry.

I am persuaded that many excellent persons, if they were confronted with the alternatives of reading "Paradise Lost" and going round Trafalgar Square at noonday on their knees in sackcloth, would choose the ordeal of public ridicule. Still, I will never cease advising my friends and enemies to read poetry before anything.

If poetry is what is called "a sealed book" to you, begin by reading Hazlitt's famous essay on the nature of "poetry in general." It is the best thing of its kind in English, and no one who has read it can possibly be under the misapprehension that poetry is a mediaeval torture, or a mad elephant, or a gun that will go off by itself and kill at forty paces. Indeed, it is difficult to imagine the mental state of the man who, after reading Hazlitt's essay, is not urgently desirous of reading some poetry before his next meal. If the essay so inspires you I would suggest that you make a commencement with purely narrative poetry.

There is an infinitely finer English novel, written by a woman, than anything by George Eliot or the Brontes, or even Jane Austen, which perhaps you have not read. Its title is "Aurora Leigh," and its author E.B. Browning. It happens to be written in verse, and to contain a considerable amount of genuinely fine poetry. Decide to read that book through, even if you die for it. Forget that it is fine poetry. Read it simply for the story and the social ideas. And when you have done, ask yourself honestly whether you still dislike poetry. I have known more than one person to whom "Aurora Leigh" has been the means of proving that in assuming they hated poetry they were entirely mistaken.

Of course, if, after Hazlitt, and such an experiment made in the light of Hazlitt, you are finally assured that there is something in you which is antagonistic to poetry, you must be content with history or philosophy. I shall regret it, yet not inconsolably. "The Decline and Fall" is not to be named in the same day with "Paradise Lost," but it is a vastly pretty thing; and Herbert Spencer's "First Principles" simply laughs at the claims of poetry and refuses to be accepted as aught but the most majestic product of any human mind. I do not suggest that either of these works is suitable for a tyro in mental strains. But I see no reason why any man of average intelligence should not, after a year of continuous reading, be fit to assault the supreme masterpieces of history or philosophy. The great convenience of masterpieces is that they are so astonishingly lucid.

I suggest no particular work as a start. The attempt would be futile in the space of my command. But I have two general suggestions of a certain importance. The first is to define the direction and scope of your efforts. Choose a limited period, or a limited subject, or a single author. Say to yourself: "I will know something about the French Revolution, or the rise of railways, or the works of John Keats." And during a given period, to be settled beforehand, confine yourself to your choice. There is much pleasure to be derived from being a specialist.

The second suggestion is to think as well as to read. I know people who read and read, and for all the good it does them they might just as well cut bread-and-butter. They take to reading as better men take to drink. They fly through the shires of literature on a motorcar, their sole object being motion. They will tell you how many books they have read in a year.

Unless you give at least forty-five minutes to careful, fatiguing reflection (it is an awful bore at first) upon what you are reading, your ninety minutes of a night are chiefly wasted. This means that your pace will be slow.

Never mind.

Forget the goal; think only of the surrounding country; and after a period, perhaps when you least expect it, you will suddenly find yourself in a lovely town on a hill.

Chapter XII

Dangers to Avoid

I cannot terminate these hints, often I fear too didactic and abrupt, upon the full use of one's time to the great end of living (as distinguished from vegetating) without briefly referring to certain dangers which lie in wait for the sincere aspirant towards life. The first is the terrible danger of becoming that most odious and least supportable of persons--a prig. Now a prig is a pert fellow who gives himself airs of superior wisdom. A prig is a pompous fool who has gone out for a ceremonial walk, and without knowing it has lost an important part of his attire, namely, his sense of humour. A prig is a tedious individual who, having made a discovery, is so impressed by his discovery that he is capable of being gravely displeased because the entire world is not also impressed by it. Unconsciously to become a prig is an easy and a fatal thing.

Hence, when one sets forth on the enterprise of using all one's time, it is just as well to remember that one's own time, and not other people's time, is the material with which one has to deal; that the earth rolled on pretty comfortably before one began to balance a budget of the hours, and that it will continue to roll on pretty comfortably whether or not one succeeds in one's new role of chancellor of the exchequer of time. It is as well not to chatter too much about what one is doing, and not to betray a too-pained sadness at the spectacle of a whole world deliberately wasting so many hours out of every day, and therefore never really living. It will be found, ultimately, that in taking care of one's self one has quite all one can do.

Another danger is the danger of being tied to a programme like a slave to a chariot. One's programme must not be allowed to run away with one. It must be respected, but it must not be worshipped as a fetish. A programme of daily employ is not a religion.

This seems obvious. Yet I know men whose lives are a burden to themselves and a distressing burden to their relatives and friends simply because they have failed to appreciate the obvious. "Oh, no," I have heard the martyred wife exclaim, "Arthur always takes the dog out for exercise at eight o'clock and he always begins to read at a quarter to nine. So it's quite out of the question that we should. . ." etc., etc. And the note of absolute finality in that plaintive voice reveals the unsuspected and ridiculous tragedy of a career.

On the other hand, a programme is a programme. And unless it is treated with deference it ceases to be anything but a poor joke. To treat one's programme with exactly the right amount of deference, to live with not too much and not too little elasticity, is scarcely the simple affair it may appear to the inexperienced.

And still another danger is the danger of developing a policy of rush, of being gradually more and more obsessed by what one has to do next. In this way one may come to exist as in a prison, and ones life may cease to be one's own. One may take the dog out for a walk at eight o'clock, and meditate the whole time on the fact that one must begin to read at a quarter to nine, and that one must not be late.

And the occasional deliberate breaking of one's programme will not help to mend matters. The evil springs not from persisting without elasticity in what one has attempted, but from originally attempting too much, from filling one's programme till it runs over. The only cure is to reconstitute the programme, and to attempt less.

But the appetite for knowledge grows by what it feeds on, and there are men who come to like a constant breathless hurry of endeavour. Of them it may be said that a constant breathless hurry is better than an eternal doze.

In any case, if the programme exhibits a tendency to be oppressive, and yet one wishes not to modify it, an excellent palliative is to pass with exaggerated deliberation from one portion of it to another; for example, to spend five minutes in perfect mental quiescence between chaining up the St. Bernard and opening the book; in other words, to waste five minutes with the entire consciousness of wasting them.

The last, and chiefest danger which I would indicate, is one to which I have already referred-- the risk of a failure at the commencement of the enterprise.

I must insist on it.

A failure at the commencement may easily kill outright the newborn impulse towards a complete vitality, and therefore every precaution should be observed to avoid it. The impulse must not be over-taxed. Let the pace of the first lap be even absurdly slow, but let it be as regular as possible.

And, having once decided to achieve a certain task, achieve it at all costs of tedium and distaste. The gain in self-confidence of having accomplished a tiresome labour is immense.

Finally, in choosing the first occupations of those evening hours, be guided by nothing whatever but your taste and natural inclination.

It is a fine thing to be a walking encyclopaedia of philosophy, but if you happen to have no liking for philosophy, and to have a like for the natural history of street-cries, much better leave philosophy alone, and take to street-cries.

We have Book Recommendations for you

Automatic Wealth: The Secrets of the Millionaire Mind--
Including: Acres of Diamonds, As a Man Thinketh, I Dare
you!, The Science of Getting Rich, The Way to Wealth, and
Think and Grow Rich [UNABRIDGED]
by Napoleon Hill, et al (CD-ROM)

Think and Grow Rich [MP3 AUDIO] [UNABRIDGED]
by Napoleon Hill, Jason McCoy (Narrator) (Audio CD)

As a Man Thinketh [UNABRIDGED]
by James Allen, Jason McCoy (Narrator) (Audio CD)

Your Invisible Power: How to Attain Your Desires by Letting
Your Subconscious Mind Work for You [MP3 AUDIO]
[UNABRIDGED] by Genevieve Behrend, Jason McCoy (Narrator)
(Audio CD)

Thought Vibration or the Law of Attraction in the Thought
World [MP3 AUDIO] [UNABRIDGED]
by William Walker Atkinson, Jason McCoy (Narrator)
(Audio CD)

Thought Vibration or the Law of Attraction in the Thought
World & Your Invisible Power (Paperback)

The Law of Success, Volume I:
The Principles of Self-Mastery (Law of Success, Vol 1)
by Napoleon Hill (Paperback - Jun 20, 2006)

The Law of Success, Volume II & III:
A Definite Chief Aim & Self Confidence
by Napoleon Hill (Paperback - Aug 15, 2006)

Please visit us at:

www.bnpublishing.com

BN Publishing

Improving People's Life

www.bnpublishing.com

9 789562 913225